From Cluny to

Memoirs of Occupied France

1940 ~ 1945

June Harwood

First published 2013

Produced by QMSL and published on behalf of J Harwood Publishing
e harwoodcluny@gmail.com

ISBN 978-1-85582-058-8

Printed and bound in Great Britain by Quay Digital, Portishead

Contents

Plate section between pp68 and 69

Cover photograph J Harwood

Back cover insets showing the British SOE agent, Captain Brown-Bartoli, code name Tiburce with some of the Cluny résistants.

Preface and Acknowledgements

This book began life in a garden in France, a few miles from Cluny, Burgundy, in autumn 2010. I was reading Irene Nemirovsky's *Suite Française*, her semi-autobiographical novel of life under German occupation in World War Two. Our French host handed me another book which had been recently published, also in French. It was a collection of personal, highly moving memoirs written by the townsfolk of the near-by small town of Cluny. It told the story of that town following the defeat of France in 1940 and of what happened to some of its citizens who wished to defend their country against the German enemy. A hundred or so of them were deported to the Nazi labour camps following a round up by the Gestapo in February 1944. Some of them were active members of the French Resistance; some were young men trying to escape being sent to work for the German war effort; some were housewives and mothers whose 'crime' was to supply the men hiding out in the woods and hills with food and supplies. In some cases it was simply a question of being in the wrong place at the wrong time.

All of them suffered immense hardships and deprivation in the camps, in some cases their physical and mental health was ruined. A third of them succumbed and died in the camps. I have translated their stories into English so as to make them available to a wider audience. This then is the story of the German occupation in this small French town and of the courage and sacrifice of some of its citizens.

I am hugely grateful to the following people and any errors or omissions are mine alone: Dr Edward Neather, former Head of Modern Languages at the School of Education, University of Exeter who is responsible for the original inspiration for this work and has been an unfailing source of support and encouragement throughout; Mady Viguié-Moreau and Camille Georges of Cluny for their support and for answering countless e-mail queries patiently and clearly; Alain Pezard of the Alliance Française – Devon for his help with the language; Tim Hornsey for his support during the latter stages of the book when motivation was flagging; Roger Lane and my sister, Sylvia Powers for invaluable help with proof-reading and finally my husband, David, for his unfailing support and especially for his help in translating and unravelling the military mysteries of the Battle for Cluny.

I have used three primary sources:

- *Cluny, February 1944,* private publication by the Amicale des Déportés de Cluny (JPM, 2005) (1)
- *Les Orphelins de la Saint-Valentin,* (M-M Viguié – Moreau, Paris : l'Harmattan, 2004) (2)
- *Eléments pour une approche historique de La Résistance en Clunysois et Lieux Circonvoisins* Jean Martinerie, private publication by the Amicale des Déportés de Cluny et du Clunysois, (Beaubery, 2010). (3).

Throughout the text, the numbers in brackets thus (1) indicate a note or reference to be found under the appropriate chapter heading in the section 'Notes and References' at the end of the work.

June Harwood,
Totnes, Devon October, 2013

Chapter One
Introduction: France at War

February 14th 1944, Saint Valentine's Day is a date long remembered in the small Burgundian town of Cluny. The date, which to most people signifies loving relationships was, by one of the many cruel ironies of the war, a day when families were ripped apart and loved ones taken away by force. Life, for a hundred or so men and women and their families would never be the same again. Many of them would not return. Small children watched as their fathers and in some cases their mothers were taken away by Gestapo officers: for some of them it would be the last time they saw that parent. In this small, close-knit community where centuries had rolled by with very little disturbance to the rural rhythm of daily life, family would be turned against family and bitter divisions sown which would last for decades and wounds inflicted that would never heal.

Cluny, like so many other towns and villages in France had, by early 1944, a thriving Resistance network. Their work was to sabotage and disrupt wherever possible the activities of the occupying German forces. As a result, men and women, unable to accept their country's defeat, suffered and died in an attempt to help liberate their country.

Cluny lies in the department of *Saône-et-Loire,* south of Dijon and 25 kms north of Mâcon. It is a small, rural town which has retained its medieval centre around the ruins of what was, until its destruction following the French revolution, the most important Benedictine Abbey in the world. In 1940, its population, which had changed little over the centuries, was around four and a half thousand. Not far away on rolling hillsides grow some of the best wines of France: Nuits St George, Beaune, Meursault and Montrachet. Ancient villages with their tiny Romanesque churches surround Cluny. Six kilometres away is Taizé, home of the famous ecumenical Christian community established by Père Roger soon after the beginning of the war in 1940 as a place of refuge and safety. There is sleepy Cormatin; Blanot, Berzé-la-Ville, Saint-Point where the chateau of the French Romantic poet, Lamartine, still stands. The scene is one of rural tranquillity. Yet for those five years these villages, woods, rivers and fields became places of violence and danger where people feared for their lives. People fought and suffered for what they believed was right in that time of Nazi occupation. This is the story of some of those people and their families during those dramatic and tragic five years.

War Begins (1)
The Nazi war machine was unleashed on Holland and Belgium at dawn on 10th May 1940. In response General Gamelin (2), commander of the French forces, ordered his armies to move forward into Belgium along with the

British Expeditionary Force. Hitler however, following advice from his generals, took his armies on a route further south and the German assault thus came through the Ardennes massif, (judged by the French generals to be impenetrable). Unaware, disbelieving, unprepared for the depth and speed of the ten armoured Panzer divisions, the French forces, together with those of Britain and Belgium found themselves surrounded. The battle for France raged for only five weeks, during which time there was no major Allied counter-offensive. The French were finally forced to capitulate on 17th June. In those few short weeks, 100,000 French soldiers died: 200,000 were wounded and 1,850,000 were deported to prisoner of war camps in Germany. Many soldiers also evaded capture and returned home, dishevelled and demoralised.

The arrival of German tanks and planes across the Meuse precipitated a flight of the civilian population. By its spontaneity, desperation, panic and helplessness, the flight (*l'exode*) was a totally new phenomenon. The weather was hot, a contagion of fear spread across Normandy, down into Paris and well beyond. Between 8 and 10 million people took to the railways and the roads: continuous lines of women, children and old men, frightened, hungry, dirty and tired, dragging animals, carts and wheel-barrows, lorries and cars, piled high with furniture and mattresses. The aim was to cross the Loire into imagined safety and rural plenty on the other side: fantasies nurtured on the folk-lore of rural self-sufficiency in the heart of France.

Less than a quarter or even a fifth of the people stayed in their homes in the northern towns, including Paris which was reduced from 2.8 million to about 700,000 by the time the German army arrived (3). Cluny suffered losses during the battle for France: five of its men were killed in combat with dozens taken prisoner, while others evaded capture. It also saw the arrival of numerous refugees from the north, fleeing the German occupation, haunted as they were by memories and tales of the barbarity shown by the invaders during World War One. Cluny, like the rest of France, was in a state of shock by the speed of the defeat and by the deaths.

The Armistice and Vichy

Events now unfolded at great speed. Following the French defeat on 14th June, the Germans entered Paris and paraded in triumph down the deserted Champs-Elysées. The French government, after burning documents thought to be of use to the enemy, fled, first to Bordeaux and from there to Vichy, a small spa town to the north of Clement-Ferrand in the Auvergne region which offered ample hotel space to house the various ministries. From the town came the name: the Vichy government. It was headed by Marshall Phillipe Pétain, perceived at first, throughout the land as a national hero as a result of his military leadership during World War One.

On 17th June, the 84 year old Pétain announced to the nation that he had agreed to head the new government and that he was asking the Germans for an armistice. The government of the Third Republic, in existence since 1870, was dissolved: Pétain declared it to be the cause of France's decadence, hedonism and national decline. He wished to inculcate the military and moral qualities necessary for a 'National Revolution'. What was created was, in fact, a semi-fascist, paternalistic system which collaborated actively with Germany until 1944 and the German defeat.

France was in a state of shock and when Pétain responded in the persona of an all-knowing patriarch, making "a gift of himself" to save and regenerate France, the nation was, at first and for the greater part, delighted that the fighting had ended. There was relief that the Germans appeared to behave better than they expected, (they were shot by courts-martial if they didn't) (4): they were polite (*les allemands sont corrects*) and they paid individually in shops and restaurants. Pétain relieved the burden for the people of having to think for themselves. They were called on to follow and obey: "regressive dependency on the leadership of Pétain was the collective pathology which marked the history of France from June 1940 for at least a year and in some sections of society considerably longer." (5)

The Germans now proceeded to divide France into several different zones. There were two major areas, to the north and to the south. The northern zone included Paris, the industrial north and the Atlantic sea-board to the west and was to be occupied by the Germans. To save on man-power they allowed the Vichy government to imagine that it was in control of the south and proceeded to erect a heavily-guarded demarcation line. It was necessary to have all the appropriate identity papers in order to be allowed to cross from one zone to another. The line of demarcation ran through Vierzon, Bourges and Moulins, just north of Vichy. Cluny found itself just south of the line. It was not therefore occupied by the Germans for the first two years of the war.

Following the Armistice, the southern zone was forced to keep the millions of refugees who had fled from the north, while the German authorities established an efficient presence in all parts of the occupied zone. The relative sufficiency of food that the Germans provided in the first few weeks allowed them to appear organised and even caring. (6)

There was in the French army at that time a virtually unknown general named Charles de Gaulle. When the armistice was declared on 17th June, he left immediately for London where he remained, appointing himself chief of the Free French Forces and refusing to accept either the Vichy regime or the German occupation. On 18th June he broadcast via the BBC to the people of France, where he insisted that the cause of France was not lost and that 'the flame of French resistance must not and shall not die.' If this appeal, considered as one of the origins of the French

Resistance, was heard by only a minority, far more heard his follow-up speech on 22nd June:

> *"I, General de Gaulle, currently in London, invite the officers and the French soldiers who are located in British territory or who might end up here, with their weapons or without their weapons, I invite the engineers and the specialist workers of the armament industries who are located in British territory or who might end up here, to put themselves in contact with me: "Whatever happens, the flame of the French resistance must not be extinguished and will not be extinguished. Tomorrow, as today, I will speak on the radio from London"* (7)

De Gaulle set about building his power inside France: the BBC microphone was his equivalent to the clandestine press. Between 1940 and 1944 he delivered 68 radio speeches supplemented by two regular series: *Honneur et patrie* (Honour and Fatherland) and a magazine programme *Les Français parlent aux Français* (The French speak to the French).

In the meantime Pétain continued to propagate his National Revolution: *Travail, Famille, Patrie* (Work, Family, Fatherland) replaced the *Liberté, Fraternité, Egalité* of the republic. Pétain's propaganda aimed to evoke the romantically - mythologised rural France: women's place was in the home helping to increase the depleted population by having lots of babies: men were to enjoy the honest toil of the land. Vichy propaganda managed to exclude all mention of the German Occupation, thus creating the impression that the German presence would not in any way constrain his plans for a national renewal.

At first, he enjoyed the loyalty of much of the population, partly out of simple relief that he had brought the war to an end. It took some time for people to begin to realise the moral, political and economic price that would be paid for such a peace. (8) All over the country, the millions who had fled south during the 'Exodus' gradually returned home and something like normal life resumed in the Non-Occupied Zone, where Vichy thought of itself as reigning supreme. The first signs of any disquiet followed a suddenly arranged meeting between Pétain and Hitler, where they were photographed shaking hands. The meaning of collaboration began to dawn on the people. Yet to many anti-German Frenchmen it was not altogether clear whether they should regard Vichy as the enemy or not. Resistance seemed futile: the Nazis appeared to be unstoppable when in June 1940 their invasion plans for the British Isles began with the aerial Battle of Britain which was fought out high in the summer skies.

Vichy's credibility as a legitimate regime depended on its continuing ability to neutralise anti-German activists and it was soon apparent that there were those who were not prepared to accept humiliating defeat and close co-operation with the hated Germans and their Fascist regime. What came to be known as 'Resistance' at first consisted of isolated and sporadic incidents: stray shots fired at German patrols, posters slashed, cables cut, usually by young men or boys. Yet for thinking people 'Resistance', which means accepting lawlessness on behalf of a higher good, is not lightly embarked upon: the active resister will, by his actions, take on outlaw status and will undoubtedly arouse fear in solid bourgeois citizens.

For those who could not accept defeat, initial refusal preceded resistance and revolt. Thus often solitary individuals sought to make contacts with like-minded others. And so a scattering of these people, sometimes unknown to each other, refused to accept the cease-fire announced by Pétain. There was no co-ordination in these and other gestures of refusal, later seen as the seeds of resistance: activities which initially consisted of distributing typewritten protests handed out in the streets, or actions to mislead and annoy the occupiers in streets and cafés.

It was an act of assassination which first brought active resistance to French public consciousness. The first German soldier to be killed in France was shot in a

Paris subway station in August 1940. It evoked ferocious reprisals: Hitler's response, on September 16, was 'that the death of a Germans soldier should be met by the execution of 50 – 100 Communists as seems fit'. (9) (The German propaganda label of 'Communist' was attached to all the hostages they shot. It was tacitly agreed between Goebbels and Pétain that all active resistance should be shown as linked to communism, seen as the much-feared enemy within). (10)

From 1940 to 1942, the first years of the German occupation, there was no thoroughly-organized Resistance capable of fighting in a coordinated fashion throughout France. Active opposition to the German and Vichy authorities continued to be sporadic and carried out only by a tiny and fragmented set of operatives. The earliest Resistance organizations had no contact with the western Allies and received no material aid from London or anywhere else. Consequently, most of them focused on generating nationalist propaganda through the distribution of underground newspapers. Contact between the underground envoys of De Gaulle and the British Special Operations Executive (SOE) was established in 1942 (11) by which time the various elements of the Résistance were beginning to coalesce. (12)

In the meantime, across the channel in London an embryo resistance network was also beginning to be established. In June 1940 Churchill accepted that de

Gaulle had the capacity to lead those who had escaped from France and who had rallied to de Gaulle's call. They then became *Les Forces Françaises Libres* (the Free French Army). By mid-August he had assembled an embryonic force of 2,000 with 140 officers, which continued to grow. On 7th August the British government assured military and financial backing and accepted the Free French army, navy and air-force as co-belligerents. (13)

It is important for us to attempt to understand the circumstances under which the French people were living at this time: circumstances which changed as the war progressed. There was shock and humiliation from the military defeat followed by relief at the cessation of hostilities at the Armistice. At this time the prestige of Marshal Pétain was very high: many trusted him as a patriot and a hero from the 1914 – 18 war. Yet for many that relief was short-lived as the true nature of the Armistice and the concomitant collaboration became a fact of life.

General de Gaulle was a largely unknown figure and the fact that he was speaking from London did not endear him initially to the French people. From a French perspective, suspicion towards 'perfidious Albion' was never far below the surface. The English had, as some French saw it, deserted them at Dunkirk, not used their best aircraft to defend France and had left them to face the wrath of Germany alone. This opinion moderated to some extent as the practical support of the SOE developed as the war progressed.

It is also necessary to note that the people known as 'collaborators' were not a homogenous group nor did they share common motives. There were the fully-committed followers of Pétain and the Vichy government, who were typically ultra conservative, Catholic and anti-Semitic along with the lukewarm supporters who just craved peace at any price. There were the unscrupulous opportunists with no particular ideological commitment. There were the *attentistes* who adopted a 'wait and see' stance. Many continued to believe that Pétain had a cunning plan to outwit the Germans whilst appearing to accept the Armistice. Finally there was the Pétainist army and police force who regarded it as their duty to obey the orders of the legitimate government, however distasteful. Some, however, as we shall see, used their positions to work covertly against the enemy and with the Resistance.

Likewise the Resistance themselves, particularly during the early years of the war, were similarly fragmented, having different objectives (12). In some cases the various groupings were as hostile to each other as they were to the occupying enemy. There were the 'Gaullists': the Free French army of French soldiers who had evaded capture during the defeat of France. Their post-war aim was to restore the Republic and its institutions; they were actively supported by the Allies.

There was the powerful Communist sector whose post-war aim was a communist France. They became more significant after Russia joined the Allies in September 1941. There were also local separatists and autonomous regional groups. The rivalry between these groups sometimes had tragic effects: creating informers and resulting in inexplicable disappearances. About 0.5% of the population was actively involved with the Resistance.

Cluny, like the rest of France, was not only occupied by a vicious enemy army and ruled by a collaborationist government, but citizens lived daily with the knowledge that neighbour was denouncing neighbour and anonymous letters of denunciation were being written by those with scores to settle. Fortunately in many cases these did not get beyond the town post office, where their intent was recognised and they were discretely destroyed. The citizens had somehow to hold on to some kind of humanity in the midst of swirling conflicts and tensions, not knowing from whence came threats and dangers from the enemy within. The witness of the brave people described in the following pages is, when seen from these perspectives, all the more remarkable.

Chapter Two
A Town at War: Cluny 1940 - 1945

June 1940. The armistice is signed: the battle for France over almost as soon as it began. The people of Cluny, like so many in France, were in a state of shock and bewilderment. Five men from the town had been killed: dozens taken prisoner: there were some who had evaded capture and transportation to the German prisoner of war camps and who made their way back home, awaiting demobilisation.

It was eight months since war had been declared on the 1st September 1939, when the townspeople of Cluny woke to hear, along with the rest of Europe, that Germany had invaded Poland. Two days later France and Britain declared war and mobilised their troops. Cluny prepared for war: blackout curtains over the windows; streets in darkness and the local civil defence organised. Then nothing happened for eight months. The greater part of the German army was fighting in Poland with a small force left to man the Siegfried line: their fortified defensive line along the French border. At the Maginot line, on the other side of the border, British and French troops stood facing them. There were a few local skirmishes but for the most part it was a time of stasis known in France as *La Drôle de Guerre* (the phoney war) or, as Churchill preferred to call it, the 'Twilight War'. In Cluny, the wives and mothers prepared parcels to send to their sons and husbands at the front: there were alarms from time to time which sent the townsfolk hurrying to their shelters, but nothing followed.

Then in May, as Germaine Guignard, a teacher at the girls' school recalls, the war truly began. On the 10th Germany invaded France, Belgium and Holland and thus Western Europe encountered the *Blitzkrieg* or *'lightning war'*. Immediately two of the prestigious technical colleges, known in France as 'Les Gadz'Arts (1) were evacuated from Châlons-sur Marne and Lille to Cluny. It was from those students that the townsfolk in this quiet country town heard about the 'real' war for the first time. In mid-June refugees began to arrive, fleeing before the pursuing German armies. Simone Grandjean, then a young girl, remembers the refugees' cars being parked in the town square, right outside her home. Her family gave what help they could: she remembers especially that they were able to provide the mothers of young children with milk. Germaine Guignard remembers the line of cars filing through the town with mattresses on their roofs to protect them – as they hoped – from bombardment. Some of the townsfolk did likewise and fled further south, possibly to their families elsewhere: Germaine recalls that out of the seven teachers at the girls' school, only four remained at their posts and on 16th and 17th June she witnessed the demoralising sight of the returning, defeated troops on their way back, pursued by German troops, and abandoning horses and equipment as they went. Then – worst of all – 17th June saw the arrival of the German armies, invading the shops, buying all they could and, surprising everyone by actually paying for it!(2)

That same evening Marshall Pétain delivered his first broadcast to the nation: "It is with a heavy heart that I tell you today that we must cease hostilities." If some of the people of Cluny heard Pétain's message, the next evening a few of them also heard a French General broadcasting from London tell them that "the flame of French resistance must not be extinguished and will not be extinguished." This was the virtually unknown General Charles de Gaulle. His regular broadcasts from London helped the townsfolk regain their morale, and it was in listening that some began to realise that they could not accept the defeat: that 'something must be done'.

Cluny found itself in the 'free zone', south of the demarcation line which went, 30–40 kilometres to the north, through Mont-Saint-Vincent and Montceau les Mines. It was to prove well-nigh impossible to cross the line legally: it was necessary to have full identity papers (a *laissez passez* or *Ausweis,* in German), which were sometimes available, after many formalities, from the German authorities. The post no longer arrived; no doubt while the Germans and their Vichy puppets set up systems of censorship. Food rationing came into force: each month coupons would be distributed at the *Mairie*.(3) Everything was rationed: bread, meat, butter, sugar, rice, clothing, shoes and with very little petrol available.

September saw the arrival of Jewish citizens fleeing to the south and to hoped-for freedom. Some settled discretely in Cluny. To cross the line clandestinely it was necessary for them to find a *passeur.* These were local people who knew the terrain intimately and could find hidden by-ways and secret hiding places. They, sometimes for money and sometimes out of good will and at considerable danger to themselves, helped Jews, escaping prisoners, messengers and even Resistance leaders cross the demarcation line, avoiding the German patrols.

In Cluny there were, as in all towns and villages, soldiers from the first war who were part of the various veterans' associations. Pétain, an old soldier himself, decided to use these several organisations for his own ends, as propaganda tools. As a result all the veterans' organisations were dissolved and merged into one: *La Légion Francaise des Combattants* (the Legion of French Veterans) (4). It was not long before it became obvious to the members what its purpose was and as a result there were those in Cluny who felt compelled to resign. Others, however, continued to support it, and earned, for their pains, the title of collaborators, locally known as *collabos.* There were some among them, even in Cluny, who went on to join the dreaded and sinister military police (*la Milice. (5)*

Resistance Begins

As the months passed food became more and more difficult to obtain with strict rationing enforced: flowers disappeared as gardens were turned over to growing vegetables, in particular potatoes and root vegetables. De Gaulle's broadcasts had convinced some that 'something must be done'. These were often lone individuals, who decided that their conscience demanded they resist the invasion of their homeland. They came from all walks of life: from all trades and professions. In Cluny the *résistants* included: a departmental prefect (6), the mayor, the deputy principal of the technical college, the station master, a policeman, wine merchants, wine growers, café proprietors and shop keepers, farmers, carpenters, bank employees, glove-makers, a priest, an optician, a pharmacist, professors, a grocer, teachers, a typist, a clockmaker, a stone-mason, a police sergeant, a *gendarme*...... and many others. All the above were deported to the German concentration camps and many of them died there, as we will learn later. There were also among their number housewives and mothers, who played their part. It was said by one of the Resistance leaders "Without women, half our work would not have been possible".

The decision to become a resister was not an easy one to make. Pétain had taken control of the moral high ground. In the country there was at that time a climate of submission, bred by the media and by the Catholic Church.

18

To go against the tide of the consensus must have seemed to some, a dangerous or even absurd thing to do. (7)

So in Cluny it began following General de Gaulle's broadcast, with a group of three: a builder, René Darfeuille; one of his workmen Gabriel Corget and Antoine Moreau, a café proprietor. In the months that followed others joined them: men and women of all ages and backgrounds, either actively or by means of covert support (known as *les sédentaires*). One of the first operations took place in September 1940 when a group of them recovered and hid the motor-cycles of the defeated Fifth Cavalry Regiment of nearby Mâcon to prevent them falling into German hands.

Throughout France in 1940–41, fledgling Resistance groups were being established, occupying themselves at first more with propaganda than sabotage. This was not due to any lack of will but to a severe shortage of weaponry and explosives. Nevertheless, in the south, by 1941 there were three established Resistance organisations: *Combat, Libération,* and the communist *Franc-Tireur.* They were producing propaganda material which could be copied on hand-operated Roneo machines. Many of the younger men of the town, now in their late teens, took on the job of distributing these tracts, newspapers and pamphlets, feeling they too, wanted to be doing something even if they couldn't handle arms.

Help from the Allies: London calling

Back in London, the newly-formed Special Operations Executive (S.O.E) had been set up specifically to carry out acts of sabotage and to organise and train military units in German-occupied Europe.(8) From 1941 onwards they were able to bring technical expertise, leadership, money and establish radio contact. The area around Cluny had already come to the attention of some of the SOE officers now established in the area, operating out of Lyon. The first one to make himself known to the Cluny Resistance in September 1942 was fifty-year old Joseph Marchand, code name 'Arthur' (9), originally a perfume manufacturer from Lyon. He had been recruited, flown back to London, trained and was soon heading up a successful resistance network in the area around Lyon, known as *Ange* (Angel) into which he integrated the Cluny net-work which was already well organised. Together they formed part of the network under the leadership of Major Maurice Buckmaster, (10) the officer in charge of all the SOE agents in France. A report sent back to London (loosely translated here) says the following:

> "this area should, in principal and as far as possible, be free from enemy excursions, at least with regard to the fifth column. The region lends itself to the following conditions: easy means of ensuring supplies, a society where everyone knows

everyone else (including possible collaborators). In this region it is possible to receive and distribute arms, train, equip and educate the motorised *Maquis*..... routes should be safe". (11)

Marchand later moved on to the Saint Etienne region to set up another network, known as 'Nicolas'. Another English captain, A.J. Brown-Bartoli, 'Tiburce' or 'Toto', (12) replaced him. He landed by parachute near Angers, in the Loire in October 1943 and arrived in Cluny via the Resistance 'HQ' in Lyon. He continued 'Arthur's' mission to organise the Resistance in Cluny and its environs. Two local men, Jean Renaud (13) and J.L. Delorme were his deputies. Henriette Alix, widow of Jean Alix, says of her husband:

> "There were two names which often came up in his conversation: one was Arthur (the commander responsible for the Resistance network 'Buckmaster', in the region) and who would become their chief and also 'Toto' (short for Tiburce, the pseudonym of another English agent) and who became a god for Jean."

Cluny received its first parachute drop of arms and equipment in October 1942. It was on the way to becoming a major centre of Resistance in southern, rural France.

Germans in the South

In November 1942, following the Allied invasion of North Africa and fearing a possible invasion by sea from the south, the Germans occupied the hitherto 'free' two-fifths of Vichy France. The demarcation line existed no longer. On 11th November (a fateful date) Germaine Guignard remembers the long line of motorised German vehicles passing through the town on their way south.

It was not long before the activities of the Resistance became known to the German forces and a garrison was established in the boys' school. The *Kommandant,* a German colonel, installed himself in the *Hôtel de la Gare* (Station Hotel). Gestapo agents began to infiltrate the town. Letters of denunciation (14) were encouraged by the government but in Cluny they were up against a post office where such letters somehow managed to become mislaid and not reach their destinations!

Forced Labour (*Service du Travail Obligatoire*)

In May 1942 the Nazi organiser of Labour, Fritz Sauckel, demanded 250,000 workers from France to work in factories and farms in Germany, to replace the thousands of men now in arms. Vichy responded with a scheme whereby for every three workers sent to Germany one French prisoner of war would be returned: it was thus known as *La Relève* (Relief). Despite patriotic posters and Vichy propaganda the scheme failed to attract anywhere near the numbers demanded by Germany and so in February 1942 the demand was no longer voluntary but obligatory for all male twenty-year olds. This law was heavily but erratically policed and occasioned the biggest climate of revolt among the population since the Occupation began. It was known as *Service du Travail Obligatoire* or STO).

> STO was a forcing-house of resistance. The Resistance movement in the south, recently unified into the MUR (United Resistance Movement) were taken by surprise. Young men disappeared of their own accord in to the *maquis,* the term, commonly used in Corsica, for dense and stunted mountain undergrowth. Within little more than a month, 'taking to the *maquis'* was a common phrase, followed quickly by a shift in meaning to indicate not just the terrain but bands of men living in the wild, either merely hiding, or forming units of resistance which became known as the *maquis.* (15)

The STO caused the departure into hiding of nearly two hundred thousand young men. They disappeared from the villages, the towns: they hid in sparsely populated areas, the forests and mountains and where possible helped on the farms to earn their keep. They formed themselves into groups and joined the Resistance. The women in the households and shops supplied them with food.

The first *maquis* from Cluny were helped by the older men of the town who were already part of the Resistance, working with their SOE agent, 'Toto'. Jean Alix, whose story we shall hear later through the words of his widow, was one of the first *maquisards*. He found a deserted farm at Crue, lent by a Monsieur Georges Moreau, which was hidden from view by the woods and hills around the town. He and his fellow 'refusers' moved into hiding there during the nights of 9th – 10th March 1943. Before long the group was 30 strong: their leader was Jean's brother, Joseph Alix. They were able to restore the somewhat dilapidated farm house, sleeping on straw bales to begin with. Dr Pleindoux, the Cluny doctor, visited them and advised them how to keep healthy. Food was supplied by the Cluny *résistants sédentaires* (people who carried on with their daily lives until needed). Madame Suzanne Burdin, a shopkeeper, who was later deported to the Ravensbruck camp for the part she played, recalls how in 1942, it was necessary to help these young men who had refused the STO call-up. They needed to be fed, they needed false identity papers (furnished by the Mayor and his secretary, both of whom were later deported) and thanks to the generosity of Madame Marie Parizot (also

24

deported) and two butchers, Monsieur Delorieux and Monsieur Colin, food stores were collected and deposited at certain points around the town, ready for collection. Madame Burdin's shop was one of these dropping-off points. Madame Georgette Colin (also deported), the butcher's wife, recalls that it was often possible to kill an animal on the quiet, without the authorities' knowledge. After that it was a question of delivering the meat. The young men would come on their bicycles to fetch it, without ration books for sure. "Having the butcher's shop meant we had permission to go out to collect stock after the curfew: that lorry was also very useful for collecting 'that which fell from the sky'" (by parachute). The young men also cultivated the ground around the farm in order to grow vegetables and set rabbit snares, with which one of them made a wonderful stew. He also made the bread for the group in the farm's bread oven. There was a spring for their water and milk fetched from a near-by farm. They were not at this early stage, involved in military activities, having few arms between them. Eventually they were denounced and forced to move elsewhere. They went on to play a significant part in the defence of the town as we shall learn later.

All this time, however, the Germans were everywhere: they searched constantly for the *maquis*. They knew about the parachute drops and what they contained. Equally, none of these activities despite all the precautions, went unperceived by those less sympathetic to the

Resister's cause: those who supported Pétain and his Vichy government. In the cafés and in particular, *le café du Nord* in the central square, walls 'had ears.'

Pierre Robin tells us:

> "During the war, we young men used to meet up at the *Café du Nord* in Cluny where the patron was a certain 'Matéo'. He always seemed to have plenty of everything and we always suspected he was working with the Gestapo. He would encourage the young lads to talk, attracting them to the café by offering them lemonade. We must have said too much and it was passed on to the Germans."

It appeared there was also a German agent, named Garcia, who had infiltrated one of the Resistance teams at Beaubery, 32 kms west of Cluny. Skilfully over several days, he noted the names of the *résistants*, their addresses and responsibilities. He was thus able to furnish the Gestapo with a list. Wives, parents and neighbours refused to reveal where the *résistants* were hiding: they were arrested and interrogated.

Having, in these two introductory chapters, set out the context of the times in France and in the town of Cluny and its environs, the following chapters tell the stories, in their own words, or in the words of their wives, sons or daughters, of the days leading up to liberation and victory. We will learn how these young men and women of Cluny defended the town which in August 1944 was at risk of total obliteration, as the retreating German army fought to heap reprisals on those who had resisted their occupation. The testimonies also tell how the resisters paid for their courage: many deported to the German Labour camps, from whence a third of them did not return.

Chapter Three

Resistance Begins: The Story of Antoine and Germaine Moreau

Authors note: Germaine Moreau was born in October 1907. In 1939 she and her husband were proprietors of an agricultural store. In 1942 they moved to take over a café in the square at the top of the town, known as Le Champ de Foire, just outside the town walls. She and her husband, Antoine, became leading figures in the Cluny Resistance movement. She was arrested on 14th February, 1944, in place of her husband, and sent first to Ravensbruck and afterwards to Mauthausen Labour camp in Austria. She was liberated on 22nd April 1945. After the war they were both decorated by the French government for the part they played in their different ways. This is the story she wrote and which, like the others, I have translated into English.

June 1940 – what a disaster: our army routed, our troops in retreat, demoralised and defeated. We were all in a state of shock. The war seemed lost: we asked ourselves what could we do. Obviously at that time the Resistance did not exist and we knew little of what was going on elsewhere in the country. Many of our neighbours seemed pleased about the Vichy government; they supported *le Maréchal Pétain*, either by conviction or, above all, for themselves and their own pockets. Some, not many, were against him and his government but mostly there were the *attentistes* who were prepared to wait and see.

Refugees from the north were pouring into the town with whatever belongings they had been able to carry. Our family, my husband Antoine, our son, Serge and I had a café in the square in the old market place, the *Champ de Foire,* (we'd sold our agricultural business just before the war) so here in the café we were able to offer these poor people something to eat and hopefully bring them a little comfort. My husband also helped with transporting some of the returning soldiers to their homes.

Our call to arms came from General de Gaulle broadcasting from London. Before long we had a small group, my husband and three others. The next step was to find more sympathisers and to convince them, but all the time making sure we were not detected. In the months that followed, others joined us and before long we had a group of men and women of all ages and complexions who joined our ranks in one form or another. It was not long before Cluny had become a major centre for the local Resistance. The first operation carried out by the group took place in September 1940. This was to recover and hide the motorcycles of the 5th Regiment of Mâcon Dragoons to prevent them falling into the hands of the Germans.

In September 1942, the Resistance group in Cluny, already well organised, joined with a team from Lyon, directed by Commander Marchand (known by his pseudonym of Arthur). Together they were integrated into the 'Buckmaster' network. As a result of Arthur's London connections we were able to receive our first parachute drop on 2nd October 1942. This brought us machine guns, colt pistols, bandages and dressings. My husband, being engaged with food supplies for the café, had been given a circulation permit that allowed him to move around the countryside. Thus, with the help of a young mare which had been abandoned by the army after their retreat, he was able to distribute the guns and materials whilst saving our precious petrol allowance for other Resistance work.

From March 1943 it was necessary to hide *les réfractaires,* as they became known, who were refusing to go and work in Germany. A local farmer, Georges Moreau, allowed us to use an isolated farm and so my husband was able to lead these first five *maquisards* there. They were soon followed by others and supporters of the Resistance in Cluny and neighbouring Blanot provided them with food and arms.

In May 1943, someone came to the café looking for lodgings for two people. We found them rooms with a neighbour and it was only afterwards that we learned that they were, in fact, Henri Frenay, (who founded the National Resistance movement) and his partner, Berthie Albrecht, of the Combat network.(1) They had taken the pseudonyms of Mr and Mrs Moulins. Our neighbours, who were supporters of our work, were aware that their lodgers were important members of the Resistance nationally and charged them nothing for their board and lodging. Bertie

Albrecht, was, however, denounced and arrested on 23rd May 1943 and died at Fresnes. One could be denounced at any moment: the Pétainists of the town regarded the Resisters as terrorists. In July 1943 the Vichy police arrested my husband along with six others. I went to Mâcon in search of news of them and was told it was part of an action against communists and all those opposed to the Vichy government. My husband and two others were released after a month, the others were kept imprisoned for a further two or three months.

'Arthur' went off to Saint Etienne to set up another Resistance network, to be known as 'Nicholas', and Brown-Bartoli, an English army captain, came to replace him. He arrived in France by parachute 23rd October 1943 somewhere near Angers, on the Loire. One of our team, Jean Renaud, met him at the station and took him home to stay with his family. Needing to find him a pseudonym, Jean's wife, Henriette, looking at the calendar saw it was 14th April, St Tiburce's day, thus he became 'Tiburce' or 'Toto' for short. A few months later, an American radio operator, Joseph Litalien, known as 'Tintin' came over to assist him. Toto worked hard and travelled all over the area: it was he who organised all the parachute drops in Cluny. There were over fifty in all. Radio transmitters were hidden by workers in the gas works from where they could transmit their coded messages.

In January 1944 a Resistance member, Jean Jusseau, from Blanot, a nearby village, was arrested. The

German soldiers sent to take him to prison in Lyon mistook the route and instead of turning towards Mâcon they ended up in Cluny, just opposite our café. Hearing the sound of screeching tyres I went outside in time to see the head of Jean Jusseau above the tarpaulin in their lorry as they turned. Immediately my husband left the house in the direction of the fields. In the case of an alert such as this, he knew where to hide. The *Résistants* of Cluny and Blanot worked closely together: we knew we were in danger.

Yet we had no warning or presentiment of the great round-up of 14th February 1944. It was undoubtedly an action directed specifically against the Resistance. There was a double agent in our midst, *un agent infiltré*. He and his fellow collaborationists had furnished the Gestapo with a list. As I had my parents, my son and my aunt to take care of, I had no wish to join my husband in hiding. Besides, who would have thought that they would arrest the women? One knew very little about what was going on, apart from the fact that one had heard of the existence of concentration camps.

14th February, 1944

The German troops arrived in Cluny around 4.00am: guards were mounted on all the routes in and out of town and all movement within the town was forbidden. The Gestapo officers, armed with their lists and led by the Cluny gendarmes, searched the houses and made their arrests. I was arrested around 9.00 am. My husband set off to go into hiding. He had arranged that in case of an alert he would attempt to leave through the fields, appearing to carry a forkful of hay to the horses. He only got as far as the field gate before the Germans ordered him to turn back. What to do?

A short time before this, one of our group, Jean Louis Delorme, had been injured and was recovering, hidden in an attic at the hospital at Charolles. My husband and Jean Renaud had gone to see him and had recovered his blood-stained uniform. On their return they came into the café for a drink when a car abruptly appeared at the door. Germans! What did they want? "Papers?" I asked, going outside. "Ja,Ja, papers", they replied. I called Antoine to go and show them our papers whilst I spirited away the blood-stained uniform to dispose of it. I threw it inside the space in a cavity wall which I could see would hold a man, should one need to hide in a hurry. I had said to Antoine that it could be his salvation one day should anything happen. In the event, on 14th February he hid there all day. In the evening, once the Germans had left, he made his way to Charolles where we had family.

But in the morning they came back, a local gendarme and a German soldier in uniform, searching for Antoine. I told them I had no idea where he could be. They left but came back a short time afterwards, saying "Madame, we have orders to arrest you." (The German warned me to dress warmly, which was to his favour). Before taking me away they told my parents and the rest of the family to leave the house and to give them the keys. The family took refuge in a small apartment on the other side of the street. Three days later, the Germans came back, threw everything into the courtyard and burned everything: everything from both our home and our business. The fire was so fierce that our neighbours had to drench the rafters of their house to prevent the fire spreading. The Germans also burned two more cafés, belonging to the Lardy and Fouillit families because, they said, the *maquisards* had been received there as well. At the Lardy's café they burned down the café and the kitchen but spared the living quarters above. At the Foullit's café they didn't get everything as some of the furniture was too heavy. But we were left with nothing.

I was pushed into their lorry, thinking that although they had got me, the rest of the group could carry on and the fight would continue. They took us first to the Hotel Chanuet, near the town bridge, which served as their headquarters and then onto Lyon to *La Santé*.(2) There were twenty of us women in the cellars there that night, listening to the prisoners' cries. The next day, we were taken to Fort Montluc. (3)

Deported

We saw the rest of our fellow women from Cluny for the last time the next day. Of the twenty arrested during the 14th and 15th February, all but six of us were taken away the following day for the holding camp at Compiègne. (4) The

34

following day we six were taken to Romainville (5) and after that on the 16th March we were taken on to Ravensbruck Concentration Camp. The convoy passed through Aix-la-Chapelle, Essen, Hanover, Hamburg. Somewhere along the route a bomb fell on the cattle truck in front of us which meant we were held there for a day while they cleared the rails.

Ravensbruck: the first stop the shower blocks: we were all naked. Some women had their heads shaved, like Henriette Renaud. It made me cry to see her like that. Then the 27 new arrivals were taken to block 32, known as *Nacht und Nebel* (6). Yet I kept my spirits up, never for one minute thinking I would die there. Yet it was necessary to endure the bitter cold, hunger, exhausting work – one week on days, the next on night shifts: we were hardly robust and the food was dreadful. Some comrades became terribly depressed. Some died.

What can I tell you? That camp, for me, was slow death. How were we given the strength to go on? To the Germans we were no more than a number in a register. Yet it was the same for everyone there. We were told never to go to the infirmary but I broke the record – I was there for 45 days with typhoid fever and a huge rash but at least I didn't get typhus!

In December we inmates of block 32 were sent to the other side of the camp to the workshops there. Soon, however, these ceased to function as the electricity failed. We were then given the task of sorting out stuff that had been stolen in Czechoslovakia, linen, china etc. We broke as much as we sorted.

We survived, that is the right word, just to 26th March 1945 when we were moved to one of the men's labour camps, Mauthausen. At the assembly point we were given what was meant to be four days of rations and then we were herded into the cattle trucks. We were treated like beasts, forced to stand up except when we organised ourselves in teams so some of us could take it in turns to lie down. There were no toilets; we found a type of bucket which we all had to use - unimaginable! The rations meant for four days had all been eaten by the end of the first day so for three days I fasted.

When we got to Mauthausen, the Germans suggested that those who were too exhausted should go in their lorry. We never saw those women again. The rest of us walked the six kilometres to the camp railway station - indescribable - after all we'd been through. They killed those who fell along the route. I am glad to say I didn't see it but I heard the gun shots.

Ravensbruck was a concentration camp whereas Mauthausen was an extermination camp. Crammed into the now disused Messerschmidt factory there we slept on the ground, on straw and if we hadn't suffered enough, every day we had to climb the 186 steps to the quarry to go into the forest and cut down branches from the pine trees. One day we were sent to clear the railway yard at Amstetten which had been crushed by the allied bombing the evening before. Several comrades had been killed: the wagons were piled one on top of the other – horrendous.

The Return

One day, we were told, "You women, get ready, you are going home." Sceptical, we assembled our bits of belongings. Then we were led to the showers underground. Many among us thought the same "That's it, we're going to be gassed," especially as the next room was full of men looking no more than skeletons, with just a piece of cloth on their backs as clothing: they had come from what was known as the Russian camp. There's little doubt that they would finish in the gas chambers. Why not us? We were classed *Nacht und Nebel,* remember. The next day, the 22nd April, Red Cross lorries were waiting for us. The Germans gave us some mouldy bread that the drivers had refused. Some comrades found their husbands or fathers there, as the camp was liberated – I knew two who did.

We returned to France via Switzerland and had the pleasure and satisfaction to pass lorry-loads of defeated German troops returning to their country. I was in the last lorry and we had to wait a long time at the frontier. The first convoy of French deportees came from Ravensbruck and the second from Mauthausen. Some people were reunited with their relatives, husbands or fathers, who had also been deported. We were all received at Saint-Gall in Switzerland where our hosts apologised that we had to sleep on the floor of a school. But we had clean straw, warm covers, good, nourishing food. What luxury!

We stayed four days there, in Switzerland: we were disinfected, seen by a medical officer, those of us who were ill were hospitalised. After the French frontier we passed the army of General de Lattre, (7) among it the Cluny Resistance Regiment. As the lorries went by I shouted "We're from Saône et Loire, from Cluny" a voice shouted back "Madame Moreau and Madame Renaud, I know them!" What a coincidence but we were going in opposite directions!

Arriving in Annecy during the night of 28th April we slept for the first time in beds at a hotel! Before, however, there was a communion service in memory of those whom we had left behind. It was impossible for me to concentrate. I then heard "Captain Moreau asks if there are women from Cluny here". I thought I must be dreaming. But an officer approached who confirmed it was true. "Don't move on, I'm coming to get you", Antoine had said. In effect we went back to Cluny in seven cars. My husband, quarter-master of the Cluny Resistance Regiment, had been able to get hold of the petrol. Not all the deportees from Cluny arrived back that day: one of them (Mademoiselle Zimberlin, the school teacher) did not survive the return journey and died on 5th May 1945 at Annemasse. Others came back via Sweden. On the evening of 29th August there was a reception for us at the Levilleneuve Hotel in Cluny where we were welcomed with armfuls of flowers.

Chapter Four

A Fiancées Story: Jean and Henriette Alix

Author's note: Jean and Joseph Alix were master carpenters and furniture makers who worked with their father, Benoît, in the workshop behind their shop on Cluny's main street. They were among the first maquisards to go into hiding at George Moreau's farm out at Crue, as recounted by Germaine Moreau in chapter two. Jean was twenty in 1940 and therefore eligible for STO (Service du Travail Obligatoire: Compulsory Work Service*) in Germany. He and Henriette were engaged to be married in 1944. Their daughter, Annie, born after the war, still lives in Cluny and is an active member of Les Amicales des Déportés de Cluny, working tirelessly to keep the memory of the former generation's sacrifice alive. The post script is by Jean's older brother, Joseph, who escaped deportation and continued to play an active role in the Resistance. This is their story.*

Jean, who became my husband after the war, was born in 1920. He died in August 1982, his death hastened from the after-effects of his ordeals in the German labour camps. I have decided to speak of those years of occupation so that our children might know the role their father played in the defence of his country and of how much he suffered as a consequence.

Jean's twentieth birthday, in August 1940, was just a few months after the Armistice. We were all still traumatised by the sudden defeat of our army so there was little for us to celebrate that birthday. In September 1939, when the war started, Jean was too young to be called up. In November 1940, however, he was summoned before the Review Board and soon after was ordered to join one of Pétain's Youth Work Camps (The *Chantiers de Jeunesse*)(1). On the day they were called-up, he and his mates were determined to show the town, which continued to be stunned by the armistice, that they would not accept such dishonour. They marched through the streets, hanging round deliberately outside the houses of those who were happy to follow Pétain. As far as I know, that was the first act of youthful rebellion and refusal in Cluny.

By 1941 Jean was in a Youth Camp at Aix-les-Bains, just south of Lake Annecy in the Rhone-Alpes region. For three months before that he had been part of Pétain's Guard at Vichy and was even called to order by Darnand (future chief of the *milice*) for not having saluted. When he came back to Cluny the idea of needing to do something was firmly lodged in his mind. He would repeat often the words of one of the lieutenants whom he'd liked in the Work Camp: "We're not going to let them get away with it. We'll get 'em!" (*'On ne va pas quand même se laisser faire! On les aura!')* This lieutenant was going to be killed later in the battle of Vercors. (2)

After that, the expression "We'll get 'em!" became my husband's favourite expression in any situation. From then on, Jean became part of the Resistance although the word wasn't used at that time. At the start, he and his friend and colleague Jean Renaud, also a carpenter, became involved with just minor activities. As his fiancé I knew of his involvement as did my parents. But they didn't mind: they liked 'Nanot' very much. My father, who worked on the railways, agreed with Jean that Pétain was nothing but an old fool (except they used a far ruder word)! For sure, there were many things which, because of the need for caution, Jean couldn't tell me about. Yet I knew, for example that he was hiding the two new motor-bikes in a shed at his carpentry works, recovered from Mâcon. They came in very useful during the liberation of the town! As for me, I had hidden some revolvers in a wooden box under the nests in the fowl pen at my parents' house for him. Once, he asked me to undertake a pretty easy mission: to deliver a package (containing pamphlets, perhaps) to a tobacconist's in the Avenue Berthelot in Lyon.

There were two names which came often in his conversation: one was Arthur (the commander responsible for the Resistance network in the region known as 'Buckmaster') and who would become their chief and also 'Toto' (short for 'Tiburce'), the pseudonym of an English agent who became like a God for Jean.

The meetings of the men in the Resistance were most often held at the café *Nigay*. In the last few months before he was arrested, Jean rarely went out without his truncheon and his revolver: he feared sudden arrest. Often he would say "I can't see you tonight," and I always knew why and what he would be doing. When the parachutes arrived – what an event that was! We often talked of that first time, the drop between Cluny and La Roche-Vineuse. Another time a container holding transmitting equipment was lost. We searched for it for hours and hours but in vain.

At the start of 1943, all the young men over twenty were called up to go to Germany to serve in the STO. For Jean, there was no question of taking part. Therefore it was necessary to find a hiding place and that wasn't easy. Eventually, in March, he found a farm at Montepinet near Blanot. With him were Théophile Chevillon, François Gargaud, François Boilly, Robert Bonin. Antoine Moreau was up there as well, at Crue, helping to get them organised. The following day they were joined by a dozen others, including his brother, Joseph, who was designated chief. Before long they became even more numerous, provided with food by sympathisers in Cluny but with very few arms. However, it was not long before they were denounced and forced to move elsewhere: to Mont, near Cortevaix. You can imagine that during winter life was often very difficult up in the woods. As by December 1943 all seemed to be going well, Jean had got into the habit of coming down to see his parents in Cluny. He hid in the barn, avoiding the *milice* who he knew were numerous in the town. We were preparing for our wedding and at the beginning of 1944 we published the bans: the great day was fixed for the 5th March.

On February 14th, the day of the arrests, I was staying with my aunt at Saint-Fons, on the outskirts of Lyon. I had gone to see about the dress I was making for her to wear at our wedding. I was on my way back to Cluny on the 15th and when I changed trains I heard the railwaymen talking about a round-up the previous day at Cluny. It all sounded very vague and I was far from imagining the worst. When I arrived at Cluny, however, Father Roquet was waiting for me. "My poor Henriette, Nanot has been arrested." What news for a future bride! The Germans had taken not only my fiancé but his father as well, who was an invalid, and who walked with great difficulty because of a dislocated hip. However, no-one gave up hope. We would see them, at worst, in prison for a while. We imagined that even father would be released soon because of his infirmity. How could we imagine the sufferings they were to undergo? Once the shock passed, I remembered the promise Jean had asked of me: "If anything happens, keep calm. As soon as you can, get that box of revolvers out from the fowl pen and take them to Gobet who will hide them". My first concern was to get that done.

Should we have been astonished by these sudden arrests? The young men of the *Maquis* circulated a lot in the town and talked without taking any precautions. In the cafés, walls had ears. There were people in the town that played for both sides: the Gestapo and the *Maquis*. In fact the German police had a complete list of the Resistance members, given to them by the collaborators.

Jean had been arrested under a false name. First of all he was taken to the *Ecole de Santé Militaire* at Lyon, but they did not appear to know of what to accuse him. Down there he met Monsieur Delorieux, the butcher from Cormatin, who had been completely disfigured. Given an opportunity Jean called to him, softly, "Loulou, Loulou..." but Delorieux did not react. Perhaps he was too groggy or perhaps he did not want to compromise his young friend. Jean was interrogated but not too brutally. Probably his false identity saved his life. Prison at Montluc followed. There he took on the job of taking round the meals to the other prisoners. That way he was able to see his father for a few seconds each day and so reassure him. A few days after, he was part of a convoy taking the prisoners to Compiègne Camp. On the journey he had met a companion from the *Maquis,* who came originally from Villefranche-sur-Saône, who was well messed up, but who had just enough time to whisper to Jean: "Be careful, Jean, they grilled me for fifteen days to find out what weapons you gave to the *Maquis*. Take care...". There was not time to say more before the blows from the guards were raining down on them.

In the days which followed we had no information as to the whereabouts of Jean or his father. I went to see the supervisor at the Red Cross Office, at the chateau en route to Mâcon, but she knew nothing. But at least she explained to me what one could put in the Red Cross parcels, which didn't do me a lot of good as one didn't know where to send them! His first message, dated 25th February 1944, was posted from the camp at Compiègne (Frontstalag 122). He asked to be sent his winter boots, as he'd left home in some old clogs, and some overalls for his father, who had also left in clogs; a pair of trousers, a kit-bag, some tobacco... it was an official postcard, not at all suited to expressing suitable sentiments to a fiancée. A second letter acknowledged my response and made reference to 5th March which should have been our wedding day. One understood straight away that life in the camp was far from rosy. Jean asked for some bread or *biscottes,* some semolina, some cheese, sugar, salt, needles and thread, some wool, a pocket knife... Then on the 22nd March I received a long letter in pencil, smuggled out. How? By whom? On the envelope it said "Give this letter to Madamoiselle Henriette Rouquet, rue de la Digue, Cluny". It had been thrown from a train. Thank you to whichever friend was able to get it to me, at some risk, without doubt. At last a personal letter, full of tender words that I guarded at the bottom of my heart. The letter also announced his departure, in a convoy of 1,500 prisoners, including his father and half of the Cluny prisoners for a destination unknown. He also said that someone had stolen his wallet and money. Of the four parcels we had sent him, he had received only three, two with clothes and one with food. He also asked for a photo of me, so he could think of me. "Please thank all the friends that have helped with the parcels: Suzanne Besse, the Gobet family, Mr and Mrs Renaud and please give a cordial greeting *(poignée de main)* to Gobet, Henri (his teacher at Lyon), Jaillet (a school-friend) and his friend Nénesse (Henri Gandrez). Confidence! Courage! We'll get 'em!" Those were the last words in his hand writing that I would receive. They had arrived at the Mauthausen Gusen Extermination camp (3). Jean was forcibly separated from his sick father on his arrival at the camp. He never saw him again.

Of the thirteen months of horror which followed, I know only bits and pieces, gleaned by chance from conversations. He spoke little of his deportation after the war although we met up regularly with Jean Pierre Even, from Luxembourg, his friend who shared his sufferings. We would pass a fortnight together, sometimes in France, sometimes in Luxembourg, and the scenario was invariably the same. They would take themselves off, smoke some enormous cigars (even though Jean wasn't a smoker) and spend an interminable time evoking their fearful memories.

By early 1945 any hope Jean may have had of surviving the regime of the camp was beginning to dim, as his own inner forces diminished. It was not a moment too soon when the Americans arrived on 6th May 1945. He saw them arrive but being totally without strength couldn't get near them, for fear of being trampled on by the others. Finally freed, he wandered about an aerodrome at Linz for a fortnight exhausted, thinking he would never see France again. Nevertheless he was determined not to die in Germany. "I want to cross the Rhine before I die", he told the English airmen (he could speak some English as he'd learned it at school). These airmen took pity on him, dressed him in a greatcoat and one lovely morning put him in the machine gunner's seat of a Flying Fortress from where, a few minutes later and to his great joy he saw the Rhine beneath him. They dropped him at Beaumont-sur-Oise the day before Pentecost (Whit Sunday). "You can die now", the aviators said to him, but he'd changed his mind!

Next stop, the hotel Lutetia in Paris, the transit centre. (4) At the same time a telegram arrived telling us of Jean's return to France. We found ourselves at the station at Mâcon and then – face to face! Destiny decreed that he descended from the train exactly in front of where I was standing. Lost inside the enormous overcoat slipped over his striped prison uniform, with red shoes and weighing about thirty kilos, he looked pitiful. He refused the wine offered by the ladies of the Red Cross but asked for some milk, he had dreamed about it for thirteen months! We ended up by going to find his friends from the Resistance at the Café de la Perdrix in La place de la Barre. There followed heart-breaking moments when we arrived at Cluny. First of all, he wanted to go up the street on foot. Then stop at the Gobet household and finally to see his house and the workshop…but what was left? Everything had been destroyed in the reprisal bombing of 11th August

1944 (5) and his mother was lodging elsewhere. But he had become fatalistic after so much suffering. "Too bad!" he said as though it left him indifferent. Yet something affected him far more deeply than the view of these ruins. The irreparable loss of his father, over whose tomb he would never be able to grieve, weighed heavily upon him. He was not able to talk about it, however.

Doctor Pleindoux arrived promptly to take control, to order him home, to take a bath, strip off those awful clothes and have his wounds cared for. "There is really little hope that he'll live", he confided in me as he left, "He is much weakened." "And our marriage, doctor?" "Out of the question! He can get married when I give him permission." Well, that was that, but that was without taking Jean's iron will into account. His appetite for life was as great as his appetite for eating. After a few weeks he had bucked up.

We often laughed: the day after his return, Mme X, the grocer and supporter of Pétain, who had watched us pass by from behind her curtains, sent him a box of Phoscao. (6) She'd seen the light eventually. The good people of Cluny spoiled him: every day, Mme Tarlet, the farmer from Saint Marcel, sent him three cheeses. A little later, the Emorine family, farmers at Lournand, gave him a two-week holiday with them and while there he devoured an entire ham.

During June and July 1945, we were called to Paris on several occasions. An English officer, Commander

Hazzeline (*sic*) received us in his office. He proposed some 'work' for Jean in Burma. One could guess what sort of work, and then he added: "We will have work for you too, Madame". Nanot was ready to accept but not me. The war against the Japanese was still going on out there. (Jean would have joined the English agent 'Tiburce' on a mission there). As for me, I wanted to start a family.

On 22nd September 1945, we were married. Did we hope for a honeymoon? Unfortunately a few weeks after our wedding day an attack of pleurisy laid Nanot low. It was discovered that Tuberculosis, contracted whilst in the camp, had carved caves in his lungs. At the Sanatorium at Guiche, he overcame it by force of will and, with new-found zeal, was able to start work again in the carpentry workshop.

These were hard times for the deportees: many had lost everything and yet it was they themselves who organised the balls and tombolas to help the widows and orphans. In the Bélot family, for example, there were five fatherless children, and six in the Moreau family. People soon forgot those who had suffered for them. As far as they were concerned, it was done with, the past no longer mattered. In 1971 he was back in the Sanatorium as the malady pursued its path. It was difficult not to curse this fate which continued to haunt him. The deportation had left its indelible marks.

....

50

I have been to the Mauthausen Gusen Camp several times now. My first visit was in 1946: it left the most terrible impression: there were still skulls in front of the cremation ovens. For the last visit in 1983, what changes there had been! Lawns, paved walkways, greenery like in a pleasure garden! But if there are some people who question the existence of the ovens, let them go there: the one at the camp is preserved in the middle of a plot of land purchased by the Italians!

Such lost happiness! Such memories! If there is one which stands out more than others it is the sight of the tower of Saint Marcel in Cluny. "I can never pass that tower", said Jean, "without remembering. For me it was like a landmark. Whenever I looked at the tower of the church at Gusen, it was as if I was seeing Saint Marcel". Throughout his deportation that image stayed in his mind. On his return the first thing he looked for was that beautiful Romanesque tower, above the roof-tops. For me, too, that tower symbolised hope during those fifteen months. Even today I can see it through the same eyes as sixty years ago.

Postscript: This is the testimony written by Jean's brother, Joseph.

I remember 14th February 1944 very well. My wife and I were living in an apartment across the road from my father's furniture store and workshop. That morning, as usual I crossed the road to go to work. My brother was already there. He told me that he'd passed a German soldier who'd told him "No work today". So it looked like we had a day off. I suggested that my brother came back home with me for a coffee. He said he wouldn't but if only he had! He might have avoided his deportation when the Germans went to the house with the intention of arresting only our father. The sergeant who was directing the operation apparently said "That will make one more!" This is how my brother came to be deported and liberated 20th May 1945. As for my father he died in Austria in the Château d'Hartheim 5 September 1944: "*Mort pour for la France!*"

The following letter is the one mentioned in Madame Alix's testimony which Jean threw from the train and which was delivered to her by person or persons unknown.

Compiègne 22/03/1944

Dearest Yette,

A few words that I hope will reach you despite all the difficulties we are in. It is to tell you that we are leaving for an unknown destination. There are rumours that we are going to Austria but no-one is sure: wait for my next letter, however, with courage. As for me, my morale is good and my health also. I am leaving with papa and about half of the Cluny people.

My dearest love, I would have liked very much to have had a letter from you before I left, but alas fate has not wished it. Your card you told me there were four parcels on the way, we've received only three, two with linen and one with food.

I hope that you are in good health and also your family. If my letter reaches you when you have my new address, write to me and include a photo, one that you like as someone has taken my wallet, money etc. You know my thoughts never leave you but a photo of the one I love most in the world would be a treasure during my captivity: ten days at Lyon, one month in Compiègne, time passes and hope for the end of this nightmare and that once more I can hold you in my arms and that time I hope without separation. I think of you visiting my house and my mother and see you both talking about our future.

Tomorrow we leave: there are 1,500 in the camp: the rest go at the end of the week.

Please thank our friends for all they have given to go in the parcels. Suzanne, the Gobet family, Monsieur and Madame Renaud. The provisions have helped make things are bit better and augmented the normal rations.

My dearest, I am going to end now with the hope that this letter reaches you. I leave you embracing you with all my heart. A thousand kisses from one who loves you madly and thinks of you without ceasing.

Best wishes to all our friends, to Dus, Menri, Nénesse. Please kiss mother, Jo, Fernande, little Nicole. Once again a thousand kisses and tender caresses. Confidence! Courage! We'll get 'em!

Nano

Chapter Five

A Father Deported: The Lardy Family

Author's note: This is the testimony of Jean Antoine Lardy, as told by his son, Jacky, now 74. His father was born in 1898 in a small village called St Pierre Le Vieux, a few kilometres from Cluny. In 1944 he, with his wife and five children had a café on the corner of the Rue Porte de Mâcon in the medieval St Marcel quarter of Cluny. Jacky, lives on a farm near Cluny where he makes wonderful honey from his own bees. He too continues to be active in keeping the memories of the deported citizens alive.

Dawn was just breaking on that Monday morning, of 14th February 1944, when we woke to hear the sound of boots striking the pavement outside our café. We were not too concerned, as over the past two years, we had grown accustomed to the sounds of the occupying soldiers who were billeted down at the *Hotel de la Gare.* When I went down to the kitchen for breakfast, I could see even as the youngster that I was, that my parents and older brother were anxious. I sensed something was happening: partly by the fact that there wasn't a single customer in the café nor was there anyone to be seen in the street outside. Two German soldiers, (we called them the 'Boches') were stamping their feet in the middle of the cross roads outside. It was a patrol, their heels ringing out as they struck the pavement, which had woken me. Through the curtains we could see more soldiers guarding the other end of the street opposite, Rue Prud'hon. It was bitterly cold, with an icy wind blowing. My mother went to go outside the front door but the sentries energetically conveyed with their "nix, nix!" and their guttural shouts that we were forbidden to leave.

Anxiety mounted as the hours passed: we knew there had been earlier arrests and a few people interrogated but this was something else altogether. Why the deployment of so many troops? To try to find out what was going on and seeing there were no officers in view, my mother opened the door and, without going outside, held out a glass offering it to the soldiers: "Schnapps! Schnapps!" Keeping a look-out up the street, the two sentries came to the door and drank, one after the other, from the proffered glass. The first German, by way of thanks, said to my mother "Great misfortune for Cluny, great misfortune!" ("Gross malheur, Cluny, gross malheur!")

Not long after, a soldier rang the doorbell of one of our neighbours, Madame Renaud. They were looking for her husband, Jean. But he wasn't there: he had gone into hiding sometime before. He was the contact for the local sector of the S.O.E: it was he who received and transported the English agents. He had known for some time that he was in danger of exposure and had joined the *Maquis*, as it was known at the time, in hiding.

The Germans, having not found Monsieur Renaud went off to seek further orders. It wasn't long before they were back and, using their pidgin French led Madame Renaud to understand that she must follow them. Worried about her three children, before being led away, she succeeded in asking their permission to cross the road to leave her three children, (then 12, 9 and 2) with us in the café. That was the beginning of their ordeal which lasted fifteen months. She came back to them sick and debilitated but alive. We saw Monsieur Benoit Alix pass by, limping, escorted by two soldiers, going in the direction of the German headquarters. Their son, Jean, followed. Then Madame Dubois, the pharmacist, whose husband was also away from home. Madame Dubois was bleeding from the nose. My parents thought that perhaps she had fallen, given the icy pavements: they could not begin to imagine that she had in fact been hit by the soldiers. Lorries passed by filled with other folk from the town, but I didn't recognise them: I was only ten and it is only the most striking memories that have stayed with me.

Sometime later a group of soldiers arrived at the door of the café and demanded that my father follow them. He tried to make them understand that he was ill: he had had four operations in the past twenty months for cancer which was now at an advanced stage and he was at present lying in an armchair in the kitchen. A large part of his stomach had been removed, but the wound from the operation had not healed. Doctor Pleindoux came every three days to clean and dress the wound. My parents imagined that the Germans would never arrest a man in such a state: the NCO seemed perplexed and left to seek further orders, while my mother offered the soldiers Schnapps in an attempt to change the course of events. They accepted and sat themselves round a table in the café, near the counter, putting down their machine guns. That was an image I have never forgotten: those soldiers had come to arrest my father yet able to install themselves without any embarrassment in his café and drink his brandy.

The NCO came back with another officer: "If Monsieur is ill than Madame must come with us." My father hesitated: he was surrounded by his five children, the youngest being just two years' old. I think he thought that if, after the arrest, things went badly it was better that he took the risks rather than his wife, although of course, at that time one had no idea of what the prisoners would have to suffer or of the existence of extermination camps. He signalled to the officer that he would follow them. Leaning on my mother, he went out into the street where a lorry was waiting. It was a surprise when the officer made him climb into the cabin at the front rather than in the back with the others. This gesture gave us a little hope, perhaps, seeing the state of his health, the Germans would soon send him back to us. His sufferings lasted seven months, ending in the sinister castle of Harteim, a place of extermination from whence no-one returned.

My father having gone, the officer ordered that the house be searched. The Germans were looking for people in hiding and we learned the next day that they had arrested several inhabitants who had hidden people within their homes. The officer demanded that my mother give him the keys to the building but she couldn't understand his German. Screaming *"Raoust!"* he made it clear we should all leave the house, and give him the keys. We, all six of us, found refuge across the road in the home of the Renaud family on the other side of the road. We could no longer watch what was happening in the street as their apartment was on the first floor but we could hear the constant rumble of German lorries passing beneath the windows. The Renaud children's grandmother joined us as soon as she was able, alerted by the neighbours as to what had happened.

The siege was lifted towards mid-day. She had learned that all the people who had been arrested had been taken to the square at the *Pont de l'Etang*, near the German headquarters. Here they were made to wait, standing for hours in the cold, waiting for lorries to take them to Lyon. I can't remember if we went to school during the afternoon.

That evening, as it began to grow dark, one of the gendarmes, Monsieur Arnoud, who was a friend of the family, came to advise my mother to try and retrieve some money and papers from the café, as one didn't know what might happen. He offered to keep a watch at the cross roads, in his gendarmes uniform, while Monsieur Pariat, another neighbour, who was a locksmith, managed to open the door to allow my brother to get in and fetch the most important papers. I can assure you that although that seemed an easy thing to do, it demanded much courage on the part of those men: everyone was terrified.

At school the next morning everyone was talking of what had happened and those whose parents had been taken were treated with concern. We had no idea however, of the dreadful fate they would have to suffer. At mid-day there was another drama. Every day on my way home from school I stopped for a glass of milk at the grocers shop, in the Place de la Liberté. The little grand-daughter of Monsieur Sêve, the grocer, said to me as I arrived "They're at your café, taking everything away!" Instantly her grandfather slapped her. Stupefied, I ran home and it was true: a German lorry was parked outside the café and soldiers were carrying everything which could be carried: crockery, linen, bedding, furniture, toys – everything was being pillaged. From the first floor of the Renaud apartment, from behind the shutters, I watched as a soldier carried out the shawl in which I had been wrapped as a baby. We were all totally thunderstruck. My brother, then aged seventeen, was horrified. Being older, he was more aware of the consequences of what we were seeing. That afternoon, perhaps to protect me, and also perhaps to relieve the pressure on the Renaud household, my mother decided to take me to her mother who lived about twenty kilometres away. Our bicycles hadn't been taken: my mother had put them in a near-by shed which the Germans hadn't known about. My brother had had the fore-sight to recover the keys the evening before.

The people in my grandmother's village, on hearing the disaster which had befallen Cluny, made a great fuss of me and I owe it to them that I wasn't totally traumatised by what we'd witnessed and what my parents were living through. Staying with my grandmother in the village, surrounded by love and attention, I was fortunately not there to witness the second part of the destruction of the café. I was told of it later. Three days later, the brutes had returned, threw all the furniture, which was too heavy to carry away out of the windows into the square and set fire to it all.

Six months later, when I went back to Cluny, following its liberation by the *Maquis*, my friends told me that they had been out in the woods that evening, (some kilometres away) with the Youth Club. They could see the smoke from the blaze at that distance. On the way home, the leader, 'Père' Bortaud, asked them all to sing as loudly as they could, to give them all courage and also to show the people of the town who were suffering that there was always hope. Three other cafés were also pillaged and burned: café Moreau au Champ de Foire: café Nigay, Place des Fosses and the café Foulit, Place du Pont de l'Etang. Seventy six people were arrested over the 14th and 15th February 1944 of which forty one did not return.

A letter dated March 13th arrived from my father which came from the camp at Compiègne read:

> My dear family, Please send me a kit bag,
> my corduroy trousers, my clogs which are
> in the cellar, woollen socks which are in
> the garden cellar, those which have been
> mended, toothbrush, soap, a shirt, some
> cigarette papers, and a little tobacco.
> We have the right to receive two parcels a
> month and one of linen. Alcohol, letters,
> money, matches are not allowed. Jean
> ....

In the spring of 1945 forty seven children and young people were waiting, with increasing desperation for the return of their parents. May went by and day by day the numbers of returning deportees dwindled as fewer and fewer came back. We began to despair. However, the more naïve among us believed that, before long another camp, somewhere in Germany, would be discovered, over-looked perhaps by the allies, hidden in the woods or in the mountains and where their beloved father would be found. I was very young when he'd left, fifteen months earlier, and like all children, I thought my father superhuman and capable of anything.

Unlike my friends, however, who were fortunate enough to witness their parents' return and to be able to follow, breathlessly, the story they had to tell, I could not begin imagine the horrors my father had suffered. As the years passed and I grew older, my thoughts began to focus on his last days and, without fully realising it, I was piecing together his history, by listening to the stories of the survivors, by researching material published after the war and by seeing the photographs taken by the SS or by the Allies when the camps were liberated. Thus I followed his journey within my young head.

Yet I wanted to forget all the horrors he'd suffered after his departure in the cattle trucks. When I imagined him gasping for air among the hundred other unfortunates piled into that wagon, I, too, became breathless. I saw him, my beloved father, stumbling and dazed, unable to believe what he was witnessing, stepping over the lifeless bodies of his companions. I lived a thousand times over his enslavement of fear: fear of the dogs trained to kill; of his *Kapo* (1) with his truncheon; of the SS guards with their pistols; of typhus-carrying lice and of dysentery; his sufferings during the interminable roll-calls whatever the weather, in full sun, rain or snow; standing for hours, not moving, there just to satisfy the sadism of the SS, with hunger gnawing his stomach. I felt it all.

Under this terrible regime, the end came quickly for the weakest and oldest. I knew my father to be courageous and was sure that he would have struggled on until the end. Unfortunately the convoys were constantly delivering new waves of slave labourers who needed to be lodged: hence to allow the weak and ill to die gradually and naturally did not serve the ends of their captors. Thus his ordeal, like so many others, ended in the gas chamber, (the final solution). I have often tried to imagine how he felt before that dreadful door: did he know the nature of the place he was being pushed towards: of what fate awaited him? Was there one final burst of resistance, moved by an instinct for survival or did he, exhausted by all the suffering, accept this last station of his road to the cross? I know that his last thoughts would have been for his family.

When he was arrested, my father was very ill but I was too young to be able to judge the gravity of his condition and therefore, optimistically, I waited for him to come back. That year had been over for several months when my mother, very gently, explained that I must not hope to see him again.

A death without burial is hard to accept: certificates from the state don't help: When I think of those dreadful times, I still feel, sixty years later, that I haven't accepted his leaving and death. This is why I cannot talk about it: the emotions are too strong. Yet, at the same time I feel I must make known to my children the resentments and anxieties that this nightmare triggered in me. It is impossible for me to do this orally but the publication of this book of testimony has helped fill the huge void within.

Monsieur Lardy's father died on 7th September 1944 at Hartheim camp.

Chapter Six

A Son Deported: The Story of René Pernot

Author's note: René Pernot was born in 1928 at Cormatin, a small village near Cluny where he still lives, a lively, active eighty-four year old, constantly to be seen around the village in his shorts. He was fifteen when he was deported in 1944 and he attributes his survival to his Scout's training! This is his testimony.

Soon after the war began my father became involved in the Resistance: he was determined to help drive the invaders out in any way he could. His companions in arms were Pagenel, Delorieux, Valois, the Commerçon brothers, Sangoy from Blanot and many others. For them, like many, it was a fatal adventure with tortures, assignations, shootings, deportation. For their families, it was a nightmare: those who did not live through it cannot fully understand.

Cormatin 20th July 1943: two men in raincoats and dark hats burst into my parents' garage. It was the school holidays and I was messing about in there: "We wish to see your father." I told them that he wasn't there and they left. That was the first warning but it didn't seem too worrying to us. From that day, however, Papa didn't sleep at home. He came to see us, from time to time, of an evening, arriving through the gardens. It was a strange family situation for a lad of fifteen.

Tuesday 16th November 1943, early afternoon: I was in the garage again when two Germans in uniform accompanied by a man in civvies came in, accompanied by the Mayor. They asked me where my father was, to which I said – truly – that I didn't know. Then they asked my grandfather and me to accompany them to the Town Hall, (the *Mairie*) saying they required some information. Some time later Marius Therville and Jean-Louis Fargier, who was the chief of the Youth Camp and whom I'd seen around on horseback, from time to time, joined us there.

We were then left there without any explanation. During the afternoon my mother, who understood only too well what might be happening, came to see me. I hadn't any warm clothing with me so she borrowed a pull-over from Mr Ducoeur, the patron of a neighbouring café for me. In the evening we were then taken off in two cars with no idea of our destination. I wasn't scared, however. During the journey I hoped that some men from the Resistance might intercept us but – sadly - no luck there!

When we arrived at our destination we were pushed brusquely into a small cell. I don't remember much about that night except that my grandfather needed to go to the toilet frequently. The next morning we were taken by car to a town, asked for our identities, given a piece of mouldy bread by way of breakfast (whilst our guard ate a more ample meal before our eyes). Then Monsieur Fargier and my grandfather were released. Later I was told that they had waited for me, believing that I would be released as well. Then, in desperation, they went back to Cormatin on foot, wearing clogs: it was a journey of thirty-six miles and he was seventy years of age.

In the afternoon we were taken on foot to the station, in handcuffs, surrounded by German soldiers. On the train I learned from my travelling companions that we had spent the night in a barracks at Maçon where the Germans had taken over as their HQ. We arrived in Lyon where a military vehicle dropped us in the court-yard of a large building. We were conducted to some offices where we were interrogated all over again, but separately this time. Name; Christian name; age; address; occupation of father; where is he? etc. Fortunately my interrogation was not too long: perhaps on account of my age. It turned out that we were at the Headquarters of the Gestapo in the Avenue Berthelot, and perhaps, for all I know, interrogated by Claus Barbie.

Then – Fort Montluc, with a hundred to one hundred and fifty men crammed into one hut, I was the youngest. We had beds, three meals a day, no activity apart from a walk around the exercise yard, single file, during the afternoon. In the evening some of the men played cards and chatted. I was too young to take part and so I found myself anxious and alone. Each day the Germans would come and take prisoners away: they returned, sometimes days afterwards and some came back on a stretcher. Everyone seemed resigned yet tormented by their fate. Whilst I was there I made friends with another young man. He was in a terrible state. He'd been interrogated several times and his face and body were bruised and swollen. It was a dreadful shock to see him like that and I wondered if it could happen to me.

The two men from Cormatin who were arrested the same day as me seemed to fit in much more easily than everyone else. One heard it whispered that they were *les mouchards,* the 'sneaks': I remembered papa's advice – 'listen and say nothing'. Sometimes there was a call for prisoners 'with their luggage'. Where were they going? Were they being liberated?

One evening we heard the sounds of machine gun fire. The Germans burst into the hut shouting "Los, Los, Schnell!" I understood some German, they were suggesting that two prisoners had not returned after the afternoon exercise and had hidden themselves somewhere in the yard. They were trying to escape – impossible at Montluc, where there was first a high wall, then a perimeter road which was constantly patrolled by the Germans and their dogs, searchlights and then a second wall. We were ordered to leave the hut and stand in rows of five in front of armed soldiers. Therville whispered "It's a firing squad, they are going to take hostages". He'd been in the first war, so he knew what was going on but as for me, I was terrified. The officers talked among themselves for what seemed like ages. After more shouting at us, which by now was becoming familiar, we were ordered back inside where we went more quickly than we had gone out such was the relief! In such a situation thoughts tumble through one's head. The next day the debates were in full swing: the two men were, it appeared, officers in a Resistance team. Had they got accomplices among us who, while supper was being distributed had slipped out without the Germans noticing?

During my internment I received two parcels from the Red Cross and I was able to send a note to my family. I spent a lot of time thinking about my parents. Had they been arrested? Nothing filtered through to me. I hadn't had to submit to a further interrogation happily for me and for my father's companions as I would almost certainly have talked of them had I been tortured.

I was still there at Christmas when I remember that the Germans shouted and sang all night long. For me at fifteen and a half, Christmas was something marvellous. But here I was, a prisoner and a long way from my parents. As a Catholic I prayed to the Virgin Mary that nothing awful happened. At the beginning of January 1944, I can't remember the exact date, Therville, Fargier, myself and several others were called 'with luggage'. Liberation? No, but destination unknown. Some people talked of Compiègne where in fact we were sent - to Camp Royallieu.(1) I was given the number 22353.

It was now possible for us to move around without fear of being interrogated. The routine was much the same as at Montluc, no activity apart from daily chores. But there was a shop where one could buy things. I also remember some prisoners who were put in the dungeon for trying to

Cluny from *Le tour des Fromages*

The corner where Mady Viguié Moreau last saw her father as he got into the Gestapo's car on 14th February 1944 on his way to deportation and death at Matthausen Camp. See chapter 9.

La Place de l'Etang: This pavement is where the deportees were lined up all day, hands in the air, whilst awaiting deportation on February 14th 1944

The monument in memory of the deportees which now stands alongside the pavement on February 14th 1944 before deportation

Monsieur Jacky Lardy whose father, Jean Lardy died in Matthausen camp on September 9th 1944. See chapter 5.

Monsieur Guy Bélot with his sister, Janine (far left). André Belot, Guy and Janine's father died at Matthausen camp on 25th August 1944. See chapter 10. Madame Marie-Claude Chanraud (née Burdin, centre) is the daughter of Madame Suzanne Burdin, arrested 14th February 1944 and deported to the *Nacht und Nebel* camp at Ravensbruck. She was liberated 22nd April 1945. See chapters 14 & 15 for her brother Michel's account of the liberation of the town and his mother's return to the family in 1945.

Front row from right to left: Madame Annie Dufy, the daughter of Jean Alix, (liberated from Mauthausen 5th May 1945 and who died in 1982) and granddaughter of Benoit Alix (who died in Mauthausen 5th September 1944): Madame Mady Vigué-Moreau whose father Claude Moreau died at Mauthausen 12th April 1945. Back row: Monsieur Jacky Lardy, the author and Madame Lardy.

dig a tunnel, but they weren't tortured. I was able to send my family a letter asking for some clothes and some food. I addressed it to my mother and mentioned my friend, Pierrot. Pierre was my father's Christian name and my mother would understand who I was referring to.

21st January 1944: We were assembled in the courtyard and searched to ensure we had no sharp objects. We understood we were about to leave. Some said we were going to work in Germany as STO's. It was a surprise when I saw General Huyghe, who was originally from Belgium but who now lived in Cormatin. His son, Marcel was my scout chief and his other son, Roger was my best friend. We had all played war games together with our lead soldiers: theirs were the 'Germans' and mine the 'French'. Their father had been arrested at Cormatin in September 1943. On my return my father told me that they had helped with a Belgian network which organised safe passages from the Occupied Northern zone to the southern 'free' zone. Unfortunately, Monsieur Huyghe and I were only able to exchange a few words.

Voyage towards the Unknown
On 21st January 1944 we left the Royallieu camp at Compiègne on foot, walking towards the station, flanked by armed soldiers. It was a cold, clear day. All along the route I noticed that all the shutters on the houses were closed. Presumably the inhabitants were forbidden to see the prisoners as they left the camp. We climbed into cattle

trucks as quickly as possible to avoid being beaten and shouted at. As a boy I had seen cattle trucks at Cormatin station but I would never have thought that they would one day hold a hundred people. That journey marked me profoundly: some men went mad, crying and fighting to get near an air vent. Before long it became intolerably hot. One man seized the container acting as a toilet and threw it over us. It was horrifying. One man who had managed to hide a small knife began to try to make a hole in the wagon partition. Some whispered that they were going to escape, more to give themselves courage I believe. The adults understood the situation better than I, whereas I lost all sense of time and slept standing up as it was impossible to sit down.

After many hours, the convoy stopped at a station, it was Trêves. A wagon of soldiers was attached between two wagons full of prisoners, it would be difficult to escape. The Germans made a tour of the train to ascertain all was 'normal'. One of them found the beginnings of the hole. Brutally he made us all get out. There was no question of denouncing the perpetrator, it was my friend Therville. Some said we were all going to be shot. I was frightened and began to realise that I had embarked on a story without end. From Mâcon to Lyon I had imagined that things weren't perhaps so bad, we were in France, after all, but now… Eventually they let us get back on but into different wagons, this time with 120–130 men in each one and the convoy continued. Some were made to continue completely naked by way of punishment. There was nothing to drink, nothing to eat. At Trêves we should have been given some soup but we were being punished.

I slept again and woke at another station, Weimar: the name meant nothing to me except that it was in Germany. Suddenly we were made to jump from the wagons under a hail of shouts and beatings, and chased towards another train, one with passenger compartments this time. From the windows I could see that we were travelling through a forest and that it was snowing. Men in striped 'uniforms' gestured to us to throw something out to them. If we had known what awaited us perhaps we would have thrown something to them, but how could one imagine such places?

There was another stop. We had left Compiegne on the 21st January and I thought that it was now the 24th. I had lost all awareness of time. I had had my sixteenth birthday on the 22nd, in that dreadful cattle truck. It was the first time that I had not been with my parents on my birthday. How can one not remember such a voyage? The dream was soon interrupted, however: the doors were open and what a sight! Soldiers, shouting "Los, los!" Dogs barking, enormous searchlights blinding us. What a chaos in my head: I no longer knew what was happening. Having been hurled out of the wagons, tied up one to another, under a rain of beatings, trying to stay standing and to walk. Imagine a herd driven by madmen, shouting, gesticulating, slapping with their dogs which seemed only to want to devour us.

Author's Note: René had arrived at Buchenwald Camp, eight kilometres from Weimar, Germany. He recounts that he became 'number 43415' for the duration. The name Buchenwald means 'beech wood' and was known to the poet Goethe, who walked there; a tree known as 'Goethe's oak' was within the perimeter of the camp. There was a legend that said that the death of the tree would presage the fall of Germany. René tells us that this came true on 24th August 1944 when the tree burned down after an Allied bombing raid.

He tells us that the camp was similar to the other concentration camps although possibly less severe: there were no gas chambers although extermination came to many as a result of the labour, hunger, cold and living conditions. At first he was made to work in a quarry, shifting blocks of stone. Before long he was transferred to block 61 where the invalids and the handicapped were imprisoned. They were well-fed and not expected to work. He learned later that the block was used by the doctors to carry out medical experiments. He never discovered why he was in that block but was relieved to be moved back to a work camp. They were marched out each morning under the blare of military music, in rows of five so as to be easily counted. He later worked in a machine tool factory making armaments. The workers were guarded by the SS but it was civilian workers, who came out from Weimar each day who supervised them. He comments that, interestingly, after the war, the inhabitants of Weimar would say that they had no knowledge of the camp, yet not only did some of them work there but the convoys bringing in fresh prisoners stopped at Weimar station.

On the night of 24th August, when René was working a night shift, there was an Allied bombing raid.(2) Incendiary bombs fell outside the camp on some of the factories and on the SS barracks. Thus both prisoners and their SS guards died together. The prisoners feared savage reprisals from their guards but there were none, fortunately. On 7th April 1945 as a result of the Allies' advances, the Germans were evacuating the camps. René was then part of the infamous 'death trains' removing prisoners from Buchenwald. Barely conscious for much of the journey he and his comrades were taken in cattle trucks to Dachau, arriving 28th April where the Americans were in the process of liberating the camp.

As part of his written testimony René quotes his friend François Bertrand's book 'Un Convoi d'Extermination' in more detail. It is translated below.

Between 6 – 10th April, 1945, 38,000 prisoners left Buchenwald camp and were thrown onto the roads and railways. The convoy of which René Pernot was a member left Buchenwald on April 7th and arrived at Dachau on 28th

April after having 'wandered' 760 kms between Germany and Czechoslovakia. They were stationary for a total of eleven and a half days out of the twenty-one. Conditions were atrocious. The train was made up of 50 cattle trucks, both covered and uncovered, plus a passenger carriage for the *commandant* and SS officers. By the end there were only 39 trucks, given the number of deaths en route. There was no water, virtually no food: research later showed it was the equivalent of 90 calories per day. Of the 5009 counted on departure 73 were shot on the march between Buchenwald and Weimar station: 1090 died between Weimar and Dachau, 793 were buried or burned at Nammering, 2310 were found dead in the train at Dachau. Thus 84% of the convoy died. The 816 registered as arriving at Dachau were those in three convoys arriving a few hours apart. Half of them succumbed between the liberation of the camp and being repatriated to France.

Liberation

28th April 1945: I had survived the 'death trains' which had left Buchenwald, arrived at Dachau and was liberated by the Americans.Very tired, I slept to my heart's content. On May 7th I addressed a letter to my parents to tell them that I was alive and that I had received their letter of January 10th on 1st April just after having left Buchenwald. "All's well", I wrote. But not for long:typhus then raged through the prisoners' ranks, causing more deaths than the SS, despite our having been vaccinated. I went down with it on 23rd May but was not hospitalised until 6th June after my medical examination. My memory of that time isn't good but I remember having a heavy fever, a bad headache, being delirious, having nightmares - all for having drunk some milk. Typhus was certainly another form of extermination: by a miracle I survived.

I was able to get word to my parents on June 24th via a soldier going on leave: they had had no news of me for a month. For those who recovered from typhus, the place chosen for our convalescence was on the banks of Lake Constance, in the sunshine and among people who smiled! Life was beginning to be good once more. Then there was the most wonderful surprise: my father accompanied by Phillipe Comte from Cormatin and a friend of his from the Resistance, arrived. My father had come to find me under the authorisation of General de Lattre de Tassigny. Our eyes met, and we threw ourselves into each other's arms. He told me of the death of my grandmother, brought about by grief. She loved me very much and I her. I had wonderful memories of holidays with my cousins in the little village where she lived. Would I find my infant soul once more after such a tragic time?

The day after our reunion I arrived in France once more, by car. Incapable of speech, I lived in a dream. I had been fortunate enough to come straight home rather than via the Centre at the Hotel Lutetia in Paris but it meant that I was unable to exchange addresses with my companions which I regretted.

There was a minor problem at the Swiss frontier, the customs officers did not wish to let me pass because I didn't have my certificate of delousing! For sure I looked like a scarecrow, no hair, the striped trousers of a convict (which I still possess), German army issue camouflage jacket, Russian front boots - eventually we were let through into France.

Everyone at home was very happy, my parents probably more than me: I was, after such a time, still stunned. They wanted to see me take up normal life again but responding to questions exhausted me. I needed above all to sleep. I thought without ceasing of my companions who disappeared: to have rubbed shoulders daily with death. It seemed that nothing could touch me after that, but the emotions needed to re-surface for one to become a human being again.

At the liberation of the camp, although having been lavish with their care, the Americans were not able to take away from us the sense of death and the talons of that abominable Nazi eagle. Too many deportees died after having been liberated. The cost was terrible: 5082 deportees left, 816 survived and then only 400 after the ravages of typhus took the rest.

The research done by my friend François Bertrand for his book *Convois d'Extermination Buchenwald-Dachau* ('Convoys of Extermination Buchenwald-Dachau') traces the history of the convoys that left Buchenwald in 1945. In 2005 there were 27 survivors left of the two convoys who left Buchenwald for Dachau on 28th April. (2) By means of these testimonies our hope is that the voices of our companions, now forever silent, might be heard again. To cry out the truth for those who perished should be our duty, we who escaped from those Nazi camps.

Chapter Seven

A Bystander's Story: Robert Chanut

Author's note: Robert Chanut was twenty in when he became caught up in the debacle of February 14th 1944 and deported simply for being in the wrong place at the wrong time. He now lives in quiet retirement in Besançon, in the Jura region, to the east of Burgundy. This is his story.

That February 14th was bitter cold. The ground was frozen solid and it was trying to snow as I made my way to the railway station to catch the early morning train to Mâcon. I lived with my parents a little way outside Cluny so needed to cross the town. I soon found it was impossible, however without being intercepted and stopped at one of the many barriers which had been erected at all the principal cross roads. Furthermore, Nazi soldiers had completely encircled the town-centre even at five o'clock in the morning, with their patrols visible in the surrounding countryside: the encirclement was total and there was absolutely no way through. Cluny was about to witness a most tragic day, yet not one of its inhabitants had any idea of the reprisals about to begin.

The operation had been meticulously planned by the Gestapo at Lyon, under the direction of the sinister Barbie(1): the post office had been taken over and all communications with the outside world cut. The Gestapo had also enlisted the help of the local French police. A round-up of all the people accused of aiding the Resistance, very active in the Cluny area, was about to begin. A list of its members had been passed to the Gestapo by their collaborators in the area and had then been presented to the local police who now had the unenviable task of leading the German patrols to the homes of these patriots. There would be no respect for rank: all levels of society would find themselves the subject of Nazi reprisals.

The first round of arrests was affected swiftly. Some of the men of the Resistance were away from home or had escaped into hiding, so their wives were taken in their place. Some couples were taken together. Other arrests took place as part of a collective reprisal which is how I came to be arrested. I happened by chance to be at the wrong place at the wrong time and so found myself forced into one of their lorries.

Having left home early and having been unable to either reach the station or return home, I had gone into the Abbey hotel in the town square to warm up. I had been refused passage at the first barrier I encountered: I was then turned back at the second barrier at the Porte des Près which must have been erected since I had left home half an hour earlier. Forced back into the town-centre, I now tried various side streets as a way out of town but each time was faced with soldiers scrupulously guarding all possible escape routes. The trap had been well and truly closed. Chilled to the bone having been out in the cold for several hours by now, I was very pleased to find a temporary shelter.

I was therefore sheltering from the cold when they came in search of the hotel proprietor, Albert Beaufort. He was on their list but had, in fact, been taken by an earlier patrol. Despite the explanations of his wife, this second patrol insisted on searching all the rooms, ordering everyone, including grand-mother Beaufort and the grand children, to get into their lorries.

We were therefore manhandled into the lorries and taken to the Commandant's headquarters at the Hotel Chanuet, opposite the station. We were all suspects and were interrogated by the officers with interpreters. We were then conducted to the restaurant where we found our compatriots who had suffered the same fate.

Others arrived: finally there were 55 men and 21 women there. We were all experiencing the first stages of what was to be a lengthy ordeal at the hands of the by now well-practised occupiers. Grand-mother Beaufort and her grand-children were released eventually after repeated requests. At the end of the afternoon, the order was given to leave: There was a coach for the women and lorries for the men: loading up was done quickly while bystanders - protesting but helpless witnesses to this painful scene, - were dispersed by means of gun shots fired to impress and frighten them

The convoy set off with a reinforced guard. Where were we going? No-one knew. Night had fallen by the time we arrived in Lyon. The women were taken off and we did not see them again, while the men were marched towards the headquarters of the Gestapo where before long they were going to experience the methods used by Barbie and his men. The Ecole de Santé Militaire in the avenue Berthelot was where the interrogations took place and the *résistants* tortured. I have dreadful memories of that place. We were locked into cellars serving as cells, crammed one against another. Before long we heard the cries of those patriots who were being beaten up before being led to neighbouring cellars for further interrogations. They came to find us two at a time, led us up a grand staircase to a vast hall where we waited for their henchmen to interrogate us. A thick carpet covering the floor, wall hangings on the walls – soon one understood why! We were stripped of all our possessions: there was some brutality but no torture and we were led back to the cellars.

That first night was charged with anguish and fear, no-one was able to sleep despite our exhaustion, as we crouched on the floor waiting to be transferred to Fort Montluc the following morning. Once there we were sorted out somewhat randomly either into already over-crowded cells or in wooden huts installed in the prison courtyard. Overcrowding, no privacy, filth, stench and revolting food awaited us. It was to be like that for about ten days and then after early morning roll call we were moved on, handcuffed two by two, like common thieves, to La

Mulatière station where a special train was to take us under reinforced escort to a still unknown destination.

At the end of the day we arrived at camp Royallieu at Compiègne. This was Frontstalag 122 and it was from here that the convoys left for the death camps but that was something we did not yet know. I was number 28082. Myself and the others from Cluny were distributed into several sleeping areas in building number 8 of the camp which was a barracks for the aérostiers (military reconnaissance) (2).

The days passed somehow and life was almost bearable compared with that we had known at Lyon. We were able to get news to our families via the Red Cross and also with their help receive our first parcels, the most important being a change of underclothes. I had worn the same things for three weeks. As for the vermin, without hot water or disinfectant it was impossible to get rid of them. On the 22nd March there was a general muster parade: a convoy was leaving for an unknown destination. About a half of our group was called, which was a bit of a blow to our morale. When the soldiers accompanying the convoy came back to Compiègne we caught the odd snatch of conversation and learned something of the conditions of the journey and also of the final destination. It wasn't reassuring. When would it be our turn?

It was April 6th 1944. There had been a summons the previous evening when all the prisoners had been assembled, each one listening anxiously to see if their name was called out over the loudspeakers. My name was there. The commander gave us our instructions: "You will leave for Germany to work there, you will be well treated, fed, cared for but do not try to escape because if so you will be stripped naked for the rest of the journey".

On Thursday 6th April, after having been searched and given breakfast of a bread roll and some sausage paté, 1,500 men were marched, accompanied by armed guards and their ferocious dogs, to the railway line. Escape was impossible although everyone carried hopes of getting away. We were herded, eighty at a time, into cattle trucks big enough for half that number. There was some straw lining the floor and a pail had been placed in the corner.

The train shook as it moved off, my bread fell to the ground and it was impossible to retrieve it. It was far too hot to eat in any case and soon the heat became unbearable. Thirst was also soon all consuming. The hours seemed endless as we asked ourselves how long this journey might last. The pail was soon full and the smell horrendous. The train stopped at several stations and our shouts alerted the railway workers who tried to give us a little water through the circular holes open along the top of the wagon. But during the crush which ensued the water was knocked over, no-one profited from it and the train soon moved on. We knew we were still in France, however, and we hoped that the Allied bombs might have cut the railway lines so we couldn't carry on. At the end of the afternoon we found we were near Metz and going into a station. The train stopped suddenly with a squeal of brakes which threw us one against the other.

Shouts and cries accompanied by gun shots alerted us. The door of our wagon opened, men in uniforms appeared, riding crops whistling past our ears. Revolver in hand, the guards ordered us to assemble in a half of the wagon, we were then made to pass, two by two, so we could be counted. All the wagons were counted like this as there had been an escape attempt at the moment the train slowed down. Then, the order to undress completely was given in French. There was a moment of hesitation but it was necessary to ignore our feelings of shame. My head was spinning – no, surely it was not possible that one would have to submit to such horrors! And yet the order was repeated with fury. Each person was to parcel up their clothes and shoes and carry them to the first wagon, and thus it was for the rest of the convoy. The front wagons were quickly filled with all these parcels of clothing so the prisoners who had occupied them had to move into the other. We moved on with 35 men in addition, a total of 115 in less than 20 square metres. Naked, jammed one against another skin against skin all shades of society over three generations all mixed up together, social, professional, ideological differences counted for nothing. How in such conditions was this journey going to continue? We were literally suffocating: thirst became more and more intense; the pail was over-flowing; the wagon became a veritable moving stable.

It was necessary to organise a strict rota so that each in turn could breathe some air passing through the small slots in the sides of the wagon. I remember licking the metal parts, which were dripping with condensation in an attempt to appease my dreadful burning thirst. The situation got worse as time went on, some comrades lost their reason. One could no longer think of anything, one must empty one's head in order to forget the reality of the moment. Exhausted, dazed, dirty, naked, for us our dehumanisation was well underway. It was not going to stop.

On the evening of April 8th, the convoy stopped in a railway yard: the order was given to get dressed. The parcels were thrown out onto the ground like a heap of rags, we were made to get out of the wagons and get dressed without searching for our own clothes. It was necessary to get a move on under the shouts and blows raining down. How to find a pair of shoes that fitted? No time to choose, everyone must be equipped, then get back on the train and carry on. It was not long before the final stop.

Disembarkation and assembling at the double under the command of a 'welcome committee', specially arranged for our arrival. Uniformed men wearing the death's head of the SS with many dogs accompanying them. The orders being shouted out terrified us and as we didn't understand the blows fell once more. They lined us up in fives and then, when a group of a hundred was in place, we were marched off, well-guarded. As we passed a little station we were able to read 'Mauthausen, Oberdonau'. We had arrived in Austria but no-one had heard of this town. Crossing the village, away from the main road, we were led up a footpath climbing up a hill. Night was falling as, painfully, we climbed this final slope, three kilometres from the station, to arrive before high walls lit by powerful search-lights. One could see, in silhouette, the men in uniforms we had already seen at the station, now guarding men wearing striped uniforms who were shovelling and digging trenches. We knew immediately we had reached a labour camp.

From that day onwards, we were to discover the world of the concentration camp system. We entered the camp under blows and yells from the SS: a lash from a riding crop whistled just in front of my face and struck my neighbour full in the face, inflicting a terrible gash on his right cheek. That gave a pretty good idea of what we risked at every moment. We were paralysed with fear at finding such ferocity, unimaginable for any human being and that was only the start of our misery.

After undressing yet again, in front of a building inside the camp, we were shivering with cold and fear. From now on it was the kapos who took charge of us. They conducted us to the showers, which were sometimes scalding hot and sometimes freezing cold but neither extinguished the raging thirst which we'd suffered for three days. There followed sessions where our heads and bodies were shaved and finally we were disinfected with a product resembling creosol which was daubed with large brush-strokes between our legs and under the arms. We emerged wearing just underpants and a striped shirt with a pair of wooden clogs on our feet (3).

Night had fallen when we were led to hut number 16 in the quarantine block. Having had no food or water since we left Compiegne we were totally empty, both morally and physically. The man in charge of the hut who 'welcomed' us did not have a sympathetic air at all and began shouting abuse which was not very reassuring. Crammed one against another, on straw mattresses on the floor of the hut, we were not able to sleep despite our overwhelming fatigue.

The next morning, our first day in a concentration camp, was April 9th, Easter Day. Our apprenticeship began with a regime of terror applied to all new arrivals. We were paraded in the yard where we spent the day standing on uneven paving stones. Surrounded by high walls, one could see nothing of what was going on outside except for a vast chimney which belched out smoke, the smell of which spread everywhere. The man in charge of the block pointed it out to us often, to threaten us, as far as we could understand, with the crematorium. We would understand soon enough. The 'numbers' which we had now become were fated to finish up in smoke, that's what the sadistic brute repeated on every possible occasion. Yes, we had been given our registration number and in alphabetical order. I was number 62122, from now one must know it by heart and listen carefully during roll calls to answer, otherwise the blows would fall. The comrades who spoke German taught us to count it and repeat it: our new identity, a number that's all.

Lined up in the yard, at last we received our first meal. We had to pass in turn before the 'Head' of the hut who distributed the rations in a rusty enamel bowl. How to swallow this mixture which smelt of beet and fish meal? It was truly nauseating and to make it worse there were no spoons, one had to lap it like a dog! No, it was impossible and yet hunger tortured us. The evening ration was a slice of bread with a little pate or sausage which was distributed, always out of doors no matter what the weather. The only time we spent in the hut was during the night where the mattresses, stored in a corner during the day, were spread out. Given the number of persons held here, the overcrowding during the night was dreadful.

This was our life: insufficient sleep, relaxation impossible, permanent stress. Already certain among us were showing the strain. After these upheavals into another world, illness and infections, which normally one would have been able to overcome, began to break out among us. There was, of course, no question of care or attention. One morning, each of us was given a pair of socks. We were ordered to assemble in groups of a hundred. Over-looked by a kapo we crossed the parade ground and for the first time we saw the outside: In the distance we could see the high outer walls with watch towers and electrified barbed wire fences. Leaving by the great gate of the camp we were led in a direction opposite to that of our arrival. We reached a rough track above an imposing precipice and then a mountain-side path, cut in to steps, going down the side of the hillside to a quarry, at the bottom of which we could see hundreds of prisoners at work. In groups of a hundred we formed a long caterpillar descending the steps. Enormous piles of stones were waiting for us: the kapos stopped us in front of these piles and ordered us to pick up a huge block of stone and carry it on our shoulders. We were then lined up in perfectly ordered groups of five and made to climb back up the steps, difficult with a heavy weight as they were unequal in height and depth. We staggered upwards under the weight which was made worse by those cursed clogs which did not fit properly. SS soldiers were posted all along the staircase, laughing to see us staggering and losing our balance, they forced us to climb as fast as possible, hitting us with batons of hawthorn in flower. Our legs trembled and exhaustion set in long before we got to where the stone was to be unloaded at the far end of the camp. Work was going on here to enlarge it.

On the second journey we counted the 186 steps of this staircase, finding it more and more difficult. Everyone was beginning to think that it would be impossible to hold out for long under such conditions. One of our companions, Abbot Deswartes, who had been arrested in Cluny for opposing the taking of hostages, saw the state we were in and encouraged us as much as he could, taunting the SS and singing songs. We deposited our blocks of stone, completely exhausted. Other deportees were using hammers to break them up and build barriers. Among our comrades in misery, we recognised Father Riquet, who arrived from Compiegne at the end of March and who made us a small sign of friendship. In passing by the large building, where the chimney smoked continuously, we saw the first corpses which were being taken down to an underground area. The crematorium was situated in this building and we understood that the rantings of the 'chief' were not just empty words. We also learned very quickly, after our fatigue duties with the stone, that here it was a question of 'work or die'. We could expect no mercy. The SS were the absolute masters, they were backed up by the kapos wearing green triangles (4) and for the most part Germans condemned under common law as criminals who created a reign of terror in the camp and in the work places.

We wore red triangles, (5) and were known as political prisoners, (or slaves) and who. before long, would be moved to other work camps. On 22nd April there was a parade to assemble a significant group of the quarantined prisoners. Dressed in new striped shirts they left for an unknown destination. Those who stayed, (I was one of them), envied them as we saw them leave this dreadful place. We Cluny men felt unsettled and confused. Within our small community there had been mutual support and it was much reduced by their departure. On the 28th April, it was the turn of all those who remained of the convoy of April 6th to be called. We were told to put on the threadbare civilian clothes they gave us. We left the camp, under escort, in groups of a hundred and took a route towards the west. We walked, with difficulty given our ill-fitting clogs, up a narrow footpath to arrive after several kilometres at a village. It was Gusen. (See note 4, Chapter 4).

We entered the camp via a huge gateway and we straight away took note of the electrified fences, the look-out towers with machine guns permanently at the ready and the search-lights. Our first impressions were grim: it seemed worse than where we had just left. The camp was dirty, it smelt, was situated in the damp plain of the Danube and straight away the kapos who were to take charge of us were screaming at us as they led us to our barracks. Everything looked depressing and there was something frightening, an indefinable feeling of horror, nothing humane. At the far end of the camp, to the west, a chimney belched out smoke and even flames from time to time and when the wind blew from that direction the smoke hung over the entire camp. Fate had decreed that we should arrive at the worst of the sub-camps of Mauthausen. It was devastating.

As from that moment we really would discover the truth of the concentration camp system as we were directed to the work stations. Once more we were separated from our comrades by the allocation into groups and it was only with difficulty we could meet at the roll call before setting off for the various work sites. We met those who arrived by the convoy at the end of March; we were twenty-five in all from Cluny but working in five or six different units and lodged in different barracks.

I was assigned to the unit Steyer-Daimler-Puch: there were thousands of deportees working there, drawn from all the many European countries occupied by the Nazis. We weren't therefore working only with Frenchmen, the mixture of nationalities wasn't going to make contact easy. There was a Parisian and a man from Besançon who had already been there for a year and who helped initiate me to know the rules of survival. Stay always on the alert and anticipate the blows where possible. Be wary in particular of the most sadistic kapos, the most barbaric SS men and the chief engineer, Ogrist who was condemned for war crimes after the Liberation.

Despite these desperate circumstances, the Resistance continued. We were put to work in the gigantic military-industrial Gusen factory forging munitions. It was a sad moment when I was confronted with the reality of what it was that we were helping to produce. We tried to sabotage the quality of the armaments without awakening suspicion of the ever-present surveillance and that was not at all easy. We worked twelve hour days, there were the endless roll calls; food rations were calculated to be the lowest possible in both quality and quantity; there was the sense of permanent stress. All this abuse inevitably caused illness, both physical and mental from the start. It was better however, not to go anywhere near the infirmary. From the moment one could no longer work, death was next on the programme.

We supported each other as best we could, forming close bonds. A sense of solidarity ensured we cared for the weaker comrades by sharing our meagre food rations. In fact a system was put in place immediately we started work in the factory to support weaker comrades. We were fortunate when compared with comrades who worked outside the camp - those who worked in the quarry and those who dug the tunnels - we were able to organise ourselves to provide support and to keep back some of our food to give to them. Each evening each one would keep a little of his supper, a spoonful each and thus we were able to collect a litre of soup for weaker comrades. It helped us keep up our morale, and gave us something to think about beyond ourselves, but to find a container and a spoon without the guard or the kapos seeing wasn't easy.The spoon now exhibited in the Deportation Museum was made from a scrap of aluminium from a Messerschmitt from Gusen. A Cluny comrade had stolen it and brought it into the camp and I was able to shape it into a spoon. From that time onwards I no longer had to lap my food like a dog.

If one had a belief or faith to sustain one, it helped one endure. The former *résistants* had their shared beliefs, politically and ideologically: others had a faith which supported them, others had lost their faith in such circumstances, and that was another aspect of the situation.

To keep one's dignity in a concentration camp when one had to wash surrounded by filth and grime and infested with fleas which we were never rid of despite all the precautions and disinfectants. To sustain ourselves and keep up our spirits – it is easy to say it but difficult to do in such circumstances.I was one of three young prisoners but the other two, Louis Gambut and Francis Gelin went to work elsewhere. Being the youngest of our group from Cluny, I was given the task of making contact with the others when we all assembled for roll-call before we left for work, if it were possible, and then to pass on any news to them. It helped sustain our spirits to be able to talk about our families of whom we knew nothing, as they knew also nothing about our dreadful circumstances.

Each morning we were driven out of the huts, swiftly and brutally, a long time in advance of the roll call and whatever the weather so that, as the night shift moved out we took their places. It was possible to make contact with the others, pass on some news, support someone who looked all-in, to make something for someone, or mend something like a pair of socks. The advantage of working in our factory was that we had access to materials and tools: that was how I was able to make a needle. We all had our little schemes: for example in unpicking a small piece of cloth one could use the thread to sew on a button or keep one's trousers up. I didn't have a belt. How could I keep my trousers up without one? It was simple, make a hole on one side and another hole on the other and tie them together with a small cord. But where could one find piece of cord? Tear off a strip from the bottom of some pyjamas. To be able to survive wasn't easy, not easy at all.

Hope was revived somewhat by the news of the Allied landings of June 6th 1944. A comrade was assigned to the SS garage repairing radio sets and was able to listen covertly to the English stations. He told us of the military operations and we knew where the various battle fronts were. The assassination attack against Hitler in July was known about immediately: that was an unforgettable moment. There were conversations among the SS who seemed nervous and while we rejoiced it worried us because we didn't know how they would react towards us. Yet, after some hesitation, they continued as usual but with even more cruelty and spite than ever.

Summer of 1944 saw our strength diminish, hunger became an obsession and we feared the arrival of even worse times, even though we hadn't known any good ones for several months. Food rations, always insufficient, diminished regularly. A bread roll for two now had to be shared between three and towards Christmas new restrictions appeared.The extreme cold of that winter increased the sufferings of those who worked outdoors, in the quarry or on the roads. By the end of the year, many of us had disappeared, departed in smoke and the conditions of those still alive became very difficult for us all. Malnutrition, exhaustion, disease epidemics all had devastating effects. In January we were to receive 'reinforcements' following the evacuation of camps in the east. Deportees from Auschwitz were placed in barracks which were already full. The overcrowding became intolerable: in the huts we were piled four to a mattress.

Before the Allied advance, other camps were abandoned and the SS forced their exhausted prisoners onto the roads. By nature of its geographical position, Gusen was the last stop for many prisoners and so, despite the high mortality rate, the number in the camp increased. By February there were 15,000 prisoners in Gusen.It was also the time of intensive and incessant bombardment, day and night. They were undoubtedly advancing the date of the collapse of Hitler's reign and this contributed to raising our morale. Linz, twenty kilometres away to the west suffered from the Allied bombing; black smoke from the incendiary bombs drifted as far as Gusen. Electricity stations were hit and so there was no electricity to drive the Steyer-Messerschmitt factory or the crusher at the quarry. Raw materials no longer arrived. If the camp wasn't bombed we suffered from the inevitable consequences of these war-time operations, food rations, already slight, were reduced even more. As for their nutritive value, it was best not to think about that.

The weather improved. Spring was on its way and with it the hope that we would soon see the end of captivity. Were we going to hold out until that great day which we guessed could not be far away? It became clearer and clearer that Germany was on the point of collapse.

Each day we saw the exodus of the population fleeing in the direction of the west. On the road from Linz came convoys of all sorts of vehicles, civilian and military going back up the valley of the Danube. Peasants pushing their animals before them, families pulling carts loaded with bundles. These sights made us recall the French defeat of 1940, only this time roles were reversed and we still had enough strength to laugh, at least to ourselves as there was no question of showing our feelings before the SS or the kapos who became more and more savage as the defeat approached. The turning point at the end of March and beginning of April was reached for those with the greatest resistance, or the most fortunate or by those whose will to survive was the strongest and who would fight as long as they had a breath of life in them. Our trials were not yet over.

The last weeks at Gusen One were hellish. Corpses piled up in the toilet blocks, between the huts and everywhere: the crematorium could not keep pace with all the bodies. In the shower room adjoining the crematorium they were piled in stacks from floor to ceiling. The last shower we had there next to that human pyramid left the most dreadful impression. All night long we heard shooting. The annex of Gusen 2 was to suffer bloody extermination, there was practically no-one who survived the slaughter. Around 20th April more than six hundred of our comrades were gassed in two blocks where the exits had been carefully blocked while they were out. They sent them to the showers to allow this dreadful task to be undertaken. One of our comrades from Cluny died there that day. Several Frenchmen got out secretly and were thus able to avoid the massacre but chances of survival for all of us were diminishing day by day. It was necessary to assemble every ounce of strength drawn from deep within oneself to keep going, physically and mentally.

But before long as we saw Red-Cross lorries passing the camp an enormous hope filled the hearts of all the French for they were carrying the women deportees back to France via Switzerland. They had managed to say a few words to our comrades who were working on the roads and it wasn't long before the news had gone round the French group. We learned also by the comrade working in the garage that the SS were preparing to leave. They continued their dirty work, however, right to the last day.

Some of the workshops were still functioning and leaving for work each day became more and more difficult, our tiredness was immense. In hall number eight, the new arrivals from the other already evacuated camps strengthened the workforce. They brought us news on the situation which became increasingly hard to bear. A Jewish comrade arriving from Auschwitz was astonished to see me with no belt: he had two one of which had belonged to one of his fellow countrymen who had given it to him before leaving for the infirmary. "You know, he never came back", he said. Suddenly I had the feeling of having found just a little of the civilised world in being the owner of something personal: apart from the spoon which I had been able to make, nothing belonged to me.

Civilisation was, however, still far away. The Steyer workshops, built at the base of the quarry, were on a level which allowed us to see all around the camp. And so, I saw, with my own eyes, a vision of horror. Towards 20th April, carts pulled by the prisoners, harnessed like beasts on the walkway coming from Gusen II, piled with hideously mutilated assassinated corpses going towards the cremation ovens. I felt an overwhelming sense of helplessness and despair in the face of such wanton cruelty. From our raised position we could see convoys of civilians fleeing before the advance of the Russian army and turning back as they encountered the Allies arriving from the west.

It was all a big mess with a feverish atmosphere among the managers of the factory. Their departure was being prepared yet each day seemed to us like an eternity. Roll calls continued interminably. Some large groups were still being used for work in numerous teams outside the camp, they returned, staggering, drunk with fatigue or sickness only to fall where they stood, unable to move further. The parade ground would be covered with men, huddled in the foetal position who would be made to get up by the duty labourers inside the camp. There was still more work for them to do

Could we hold out for a few more days? One began to doubt it: everything was so hard to bear. It needed every ounce of physical and psychological strength to resist beyond what one thought possible. The Red Cross lorries came back with a new cargo of deportees. We began to believe in the possibility of being liberated. Don't dream too soon! However on the evening of April 27th it was announced that blocks holding French, Belgian and Dutch prisoners need not go to work the next day. On the morning of the 28th all those capable of walking were assembled in the parade ground. Torrential rain began to fall, soaking us as we waited there for hours. And then, an unimaginable surprise: parcels from the Red Cross were distributed to each one. All that was eatable was devoured straight away: unfortunately most of the parcel proved to be uneatable.

During the afternoon a pitiful column wound its way towards the central camp. We looked like tramps, dirty, in rags, covered in vermin as we advanced painfully. The slope was a tough climb, the stronger among us helped the weaker. I helped my comrade, Robert Dubol from Besançon, who was at the end of his strength, to negotiate the last few kilometres. (He would not live to see the Liberation). As we arrived at the camp we saw that the third convoy of white Red Cross lorries was leaving, taking off the last of the French women and some of the men who were most exhausted. That was to be the last convoy and we waited in vain for their return. The final battle was taking place on the roads between here and Switzerland and it was impossible to cross that zone while fighting was going on. It was a new and cruel disillusionment. We found refuge in the abominable quarantine blocks. I found myself in Block 15, the same one that I left exactly a year before, to the day. The same boss in charge, but at least we knew that it wasn't for long. The front was drawing nearer and we could hear the sounds of the gun-fire nearby and saw the airplanes attacking the bridges over the Danube, the explosions rocking the huts.

There was much confusion and we waited anxiously what would happen next. The SS abandoned the camp on the 3rd May after having destroyed the cremation ovens and killed all those working there. Their place was taken by reservists, old soldiers no doubt called up at the last moment. We asked ourselves where the SS would go. To the east the Russians were already in the suburbs of Vienna; their reconnaissance tanks came close to Mauthausen which encouraged the Russian prisoners to attempt an escape, hoping to join their compatriots. They had been re-captured, however and there had been the most awful retributions: one could count the survivors on the fingers of one hand from the hundreds of men who had tried to escape over the electrified fences.

To the west were the Americans and the French who were coming via the valley of the Danube. The SS hadn't gone far, in fact, they were watching the camp and the confusion which reigned there through field glasses. On 5th May there was the most extraordinary clamour: the gates of our block had been opened and we all ran into the huge court-yard to see a cloud of deportees surrounding an American jeep and two other vehicles. The soldiers, on a reconnaissance mission, found themselves in an advanced position without an apparent motive. They had no information on the existence of a concentration camp. But for us, it was enough: it was the end, we were going home. Some even thought we would be repatriated by air. The Americans left but the SS had followed all this from a distance and came back to attack the camp, almost certainly in the hope of exterminating us all, those that they hadn't already killed. But this time they met with opposition. It was the Resistance fighters, with their already organised plans, which had been in place for some time who took charge of the camp, among them a Russian officer. All the old German reservist soldiers were disarmed: they didn't put up a fight, they seemed to feel liberated themselves also, and it meant we then had arms. The camp was under the command of the international Resistance. The three days before the Americans arrived in force was total chaos. No organisation, no direction but complete confusion with plenty of old scores being settled with some of the kapos - the chiefs of the Blocks. Death was everywhere with corpses piling up: it was hot and the smell was appalling; the crematorium ovens no longer worked and what could we deportees do in the state we were in? Some of the Resistance fighters went out pillaging the farms round about, bringing back all they could carry - potatoes, flour, pigs - to feed the thousands of men who were still there. One had something to eat but I don't remember feeling better for it.

Then it was May 8[th,] the day the American army arrived in force, with provisions. They disarmed the civilians and took control of the camp. It was the end of the war. The Nazis had capitulated and normally fighting must cease at that point but the SS hadn't given up. Unfortunately there were comrades who lost their lives in going to defend the bridges at Mauthausen and Enns to prevent the SS penetrating the camp during fierce armed battles. It was the Allied soldiers, many of them black, who took over the guard. Some days were to pass before we were repatriated: several comrades, exhausted by so much horror, died before arriving back on French soil.

Liberation (6,7)

At long last our liberators had arrived. Days were to pass however before order was restored. One day, with the aid of French comrades, we got hold of a ladder, and climbing up onto the roof we were able to see the world outside the camp for the first time and see exactly where the camp lay within the vast valley of the Danube. Whilst up there, someone offered me a cigarette, the only cigarette in fact that I have ever smoked, but it was an emblem of victory, of liberation: we never imagined we would ever see this day. Did I feel joy? Yes, but it was rather a mixture of joy and sadness, the moment spoiled by so many dreadful memories, so we were not able to totally savour the knowledge of the annihilation of the Nazi's: our bodies weren't strong enough, either physically or mentally.

Days passed.....we saw the Red Cross and the military authorities coming and going but we didn't know much about what was going on. We knew the first job the Americans organised was the burial of all the corpses. They requisitioned the local civilians of Mauthausen and Gusen for the job. Those who "knew nothing, had seen nothing and understood nothing" now spent days dragging the corpses for burial in communal graves dug out by bulldozers.

Slowly some organisation formed among the deportees as it sometimes seemed that no-one was taking care of us. It was necessary that someone should speak to the authorities to find out who was going to take responsibility for us and when we were going to be able to leave. So we organised ourselves to leave for Paris where we could get help and be repatriated as quickly as possible. A group left around May 16th, but without the Colonel-in-charge's knowledge: he was on leave.

On reflection, I suppose that having been fighting a long way from home and in atrocious conditions, these American soldiers' chief aim had been accomplished and the repatriation of we civilians was of secondary importance. We would just have to wait, they certainly had plenty to do as sickness and death continued without cease. They had constructed field hospitals to which the weakest were admitted, the majority did not come out, it proving impossible to get them back on their feet.

One morning we were told that all the French whose names began with A, B, C, D or F were to assemble on the parade ground. Outside, a motley collection of German and American vehicles were waiting to take us to the airport at Linz. It was the first time we had seen some of them, like Jeeps and Dodges. And so we left: it was all well-organised, the convoy was accompanied by a despatch rider who went up and down the column, sorting out problems with the vehicles. We followed the course of the Danube and eventually arrived at Linz. We spent the night in what must have been a sugar refinery while the convoy returned to Mauthausen. There wasn't any food organised for us. Back at the camp the American colonel, having returned from leave in the meantime, saw the stratagem the deportees had put in place in order to speed up repatriation. He agreed that all the others could also leave on condition they passed a medical examination. Some weren't allowed to leave as they were not considered sufficiently fit.

The following day we waited at the airport for our departure. We were told, however, that they were in the process of repatriating military prisoners but not civilians. They led us to understand that they couldn't deal with us at that time as we had not been expected as part of the current operations. During the morning of 19th May, after negotiations with the leaders of our group, they finally agreed to repatriate us by air. We were called by name, in groups of thirty, to take our place beside one of the flying fortresses lined up at the airbase. There were twenty-seven of them which carried eight hundred and ten Frenchmen back to France, alive but in deplorable health. Three hours later we landed at Beaumont-sur-Oise, where an official reception awaited us. From there we were transferred to the railway station, again with a reception on the platform; we were offered food and even wine… there were ripe cherries but I couldn't eat anything, my body couldn't cope with it. But I did drink a little red wine, but it seemed very acidic and strong after so long, and I could only swallow a mouthful. Our families weren't aware that we had arrived back in France but they knew we had been liberated because we had been able to write to them. I'd written around the 12th May and the letter had arrived! They knew that we were alive but that was all they knew. A report had doubtlessly appeared in the press, giving details of those who had escaped from Mauthausen on 5th May 1945, but who had seen the newspaper?

We were then transferred to Paris, arriving at the Gare du Nord where once again we were met by a reception of military and civilian authorities. It wasn't a happy journey however. We had a police escort and walked, watched by the families of deportees from the Paris region who had learned of the convoy's arrival. They brandished photos, cried out names, but we carried on with our heads bowed, silent: the Marseillaise played on as we were conducted to the Hotel Lutetia where all the repatriation formalities were carried out.

We were interrogated on our deportation beginning with the day of our arrest all of which took some time, and then given a repatriation card which served as an identity card, a small amount of money to see us through until further financial help became available and a train ticket home. We then had a medical examination and an X-ray. When I left, I suspected what might lie ahead: I had read my repatriation papers where it said that the X-ray of my right lung should be verified.

We were then taken to various hotels, myself and a comrade taken to the hotel Imperator. We were told that telegrams has already been despatched and that the following day a taxi would take us to the station. (What we didn't know was that we would get home before the telegram, so no-one was waiting for us when we arrived back). That morning there was no need to wake us, for we had hardly slept at all: we were not used to soft beds and it felt as if we were sinking into softness without end.

I went home in the same clothes as those in which I had left the camp, with trousers I had cut off above the knee to be free both of dirt and vermin, a striped shirt, my beret and a pair of old slippers. I had thrown away my boots, which I found too heavy to wear, undoubtedly as a result of my lack of strength, and I had found a pair of canvas slippers in the crematorium at Mauthausen. They must have belonged to one of the kapos working there. They had been liquidated by the SS before they left, so they weren't going to talk.

Once we were home we were in such a state of absolute fatigue that we didn't want to talk much: above all we just wanted to sleep, to try not to think of the past fifteen months, to take things gently. But it wasn't that simple. We needed to think about work: the authorities had allowed us a month's leave, which turned out to be three months in the end. Once home we received one obligatory visit from the authorities, that was all. However, there was family, youth and hope to keep us going.

We thought we'd be able to eat but it was very difficult. I had dreamed of a blanquette de veau and my mother had managed to get some veal, but I couldn't eat it. My appetite slowly came back, however, and it was undoubtedly better that way as eating too much too soon after such deprivation can lead to problems. I took up my work again in October. With a careful health regime I slowly gained strength and climbed the hill back to health despite a relapse ten years later.

Chapter Eight

The Secret Agent's Escape: The Story of Captain Cayotte

Author's note: This testimony arrived by post in February 2010 sent to me by Mlle Marie-Angély Rébillard, (a well-known figure in Cluny and whose personal story we will hear later). It had been sent to her, typed on an old Roneo type-writer, by an elderly priest, who was by that time living east of Cluny in the Rhone Alps region. It is the story of how he helped a French Intelligence Agent escape the Nazis. It has not been published but it seemed worthy of translation and inclusion here. The story concerns one Charles Louis Cayotte (wartime alias Colas) who was born in 1897 in Nancy, France. He fought throughout the First World War, joining the newly-formed French air force in 1918, after just one month's instruction. He was awarded the Chevalier de la Légion d'honneur and the Croix de Guerre, 1914–1918. He re-joined the air force in 1938 and on demobilisation after the Armistice joined the Free French army, working with the Resistance as an Intelligence Officer in the Saône and Loire region, near Cluny. This is my translation of his memoir.

It was the end of March, 1944. Since their defeat at Stalingrad, the Germans had become particularly nervous and were tracking all the 'terrorists' (as they regarded the men of the Resistance). I had just been released from my illegal status (I had been in hiding having refused the compulsory work service STO), as had all the other seminarians (1) and I was by now living quite openly with my family at Grièges, having hidden out the winter in the woods at Montnoyer. I was about to return to the seminary at Belley in September for the beginning of the new term.

Dr. Louis Combe was a neighbour of my parents. He was a retired Army Colonel, formerly of Algiers who had retired and bought an estate and some agricultural land near-by. Having been introduced to our family by the local priest, he often came to seek my father's advice with regard to his land and he remained attached to my family. A veteran of the Riff campaign and the Great War, he had been deeply affected by the defeat of 1940. At the end of March 1944 he turned up at Grièges wishing to talk to me alone. What a surprise! He told me that he had accepted responsibility in the *maquis* for the region of Dombes, Bords de Saône and was in constant contact with the *maquis* at Cluny. He then proposed a very specific mission that he wanted me to undertake.

A certain Captain Cayotte of the French Intelligence Services was being hunted by the Gestapo and was living with his family at Hurigny.(2) He had decided that if his situation began to look dangerous he would swim across the River Saone and reach safety at the house of Dr. Combe. who would then contact me. I was then to go to meet the Captain and carry out any instructions he might give me. It would be in total secrecy of course. Without fully understanding what was involved I told him he could count on me. I didn't mention it to the family. A few days later there was a telephone call: "See you tomorrow at 3.0 pm. Captain Cayotte has just arrived, as expected".

As arranged I went to Dr Combes' house. It was a Saturday. I found the Captain, a hunted man, still shivering from his swim across the Saone. Once we had been introduced, he told me of the previous evening's drama. He and the family were on the point of going to bed when he heard shouts from outside in a strong, guttural accent. He knew immediately what was happening and so jumped out from a first floor window into the boxwood hedge underneath. Powerful beams from search lights suddenly illuminated the front of the house. It was too late however, he had already left. He reached a deserted spot on the banks of the Saone a few kilometres away, swam across, took the towpath and arrived, frozen, at the doctor's house. Not knowing what might have happened to the wife and children he had left behind, he appeared a brave but tearful man. He had two tasks that he needed me to undertake for him, my relative immunity as a priest providing security. Knowing that I was a member of the Prado (3), he asked if I could contact Father Jaillet (who was the director of the Prado Rehabilitation Centre at Hurigny) and to ask him if he would come and pick him up and drive him to St. Mercelin, near Grenoble (and near the *Maquis* at Vercors). He also asked if I could go back to his home in Hurigny to remove some papers which he had been forced to leave behind. They were hidden under a barrel in the cellar and were important for the defence of the territory. They showed details of German troop movements on the Russian front. These documents then needed to be taken in the greatest secrecy to an address in Macon. "Every fifty yards you must turn to ensure that you are not being followed. Go and good luck!"

The next day was a Sunday. I made a phone call and asked if I might call at the Prado at Hurigny. Father Jaillet invited me to lunch. He said that there would be some of the other Prado teachers there and also his elderly father. I arrived on my bike and joined the lunch party where I found there was only one topic of conversation: the arrival of the Gestapo at the home of Captain Cayotte. The Germans, unable to capture him had taken his wife and two sons. The village was reeling from the shock: at Mass that morning the talk had been only of this drama .... At the end of lunch I asked Father Jaillet if I could talk to him a moment. "I am here on behalf of the captain who has escaped." What a surprise on the face of the good father Jaillet! I explained the mission entrusted to me.

He agreed to go and pick up the Captain and drive him to St Marcelin but as for retrieving the documents from the house, the Father thought it very imprudent to go back there. It was highly likely that Gestapo agents were still in the vicinity. I therefore abandoned this part of my mission. Father Jaillet said he would explain to the Captain. So I returned home to Grièges still shaken by the recent events of this memorable Sunday.

The landings in Normandy and Provence were to take place in the following months. The *Maquis* at Vercors, at Cluny and in many other places were harassing the retreating Germans, but there was no news of the escaped Captain or of his family. And slowly silence fell on these local events.

······················

In 1994, 50 years later, France commemorated the landings and the liberation. I was, by this time a priest at Thoiry. It came to me that I would like to know what happened to Captain Cayotte. Yes, but how?

A woman of the parish, Mrs Marie-Francoise Jouanneau, invited me to lunch one day with her cousin, a Dr. Chambaud, who lived near Mâcon but was on holiday in our region. The doctor was retired and near my age. He seemed both interested and curious on hearing of my story. He took some notes, and said that he would make it his business to pursue the matter when he got back to Mâcon. He said that he had links in the Cluny area and would see what he could find out about the work of the *maquis* there during the war. I also wrote to Mlle Rébillard, who had been a nurse and social worker in Cluny during the war and who had given sterling assistance to the men of the Resistance.

I learned from Dr Chambaud that he had found traces of Captain Cayotte, who had since died, and he gave me the name and address of his son, Bernard, who was president of Deportees of Nancy, and of his brother Francis. I phoned Bernard, who was quite moved to talk about his father and those days. He had not known of my participation in his father's escape from their house at Hurigny. It transpired that the Captain was able to continue the fight for the liberation of France ending up as a major in the 'Bureau du Chiffre'(5). His wife, Bernard's mother, was deported to Ravensbrück. She returned from the camp and died in 1981, fourteen years after the death of her husband in 1967. Bernard and his younger brother had escaped by jumping off the train taking them to imprisonment in Germany.

He promised to make a detour one day to visit me when next on holiday. I haven't seen him as yet but am glad to have known the end of the adventure of Captain Cayotte of the *Maquis* of the Secret Army of Cluny. A little story - but part of the history of France.

Author's note:Captain Cayotte continued his resistance activities in the areas on the Rhône and the Ain, belonging to the team Marco Polo. His wife, Joséphine also worked with the Marco Polo team before her arrest. She was deported to Ravensbruck camp and was liberated in April 1945. The Captain was awarded the Resistance Medal after the Second World War.

Chapter 9

The Orphans of Saint Valentine's Day 1944: Marie-M. Viguié-Moreau

Author's note: Mady Viguié, as she likes to be known, was ten when she last saw her father, Claude Moreau. She met her husband Pierre in Cluny after the war ended and they were married in 1955. He grew up in the Auvergne region of France and won a place at the School of Arts and Engineering in Cluny and they met at the school drama society. After living near Paris and running her own boutique in Versailles for many years, Mady and Pierre returned to live in Cluny in 2008. Mady continues to play a huge role in commemorating the deportees of Mauthausen both locally and nationally. She published her own account of those times, Les Orphelins de la Saint-Valentin in 2004 This, her story, is translated from that work. (1)

In 1940, when the Second World War in France started in earnest, I was six years old. Rather than actual memories, I have a feeling that my early childhood was very happy with my mother and father, sister and three brothers. My brother, Jean, was five years older than me. Barely two years separated me from my younger sister, Andrée. Then there were the babies: our twin brothers, born just after war was declared. For my sister and me they were our preferred play-things, I think we regarded them as two identical dolls.

We lived, laughed and played, protected by the love and affection of our parents, in our house in Cluny. It had a large, enclosed garden which was the place of our games and our day-dreams. There was an outhouse which served as a laundry. Obviously, washing machines didn't exist in those days, and so a woman of the town would come to take care of the enormous piles of washing we managed to make between us. After the clothes had all been boiled she would pile everything onto a wheel-barrow to take to the river for rinsing. My sister and I loved to go with her, where we would listen to the rich and highly-coloured gossip of les *laveuses*. We learned all sorts of rude words there which we were not allowed to use at home!

In 1940, rationing had already begun and *les tickets de rationnement* were distributed by the mayor. Despite the restrictions we didn't really go short and certainly weren't hungry in the way that people of the big towns became as provisions dwindled or were kept for the German occupiers. Our lawn had given way to a kitchen garden: the bottom bit was fenced off for the chickens who now supplied us with eggs. My father was a wine merchant, and so, beyond the chickens was *le chai,* where the wine was made, with all its complicated equipment: barrels, bottles, racks, casks, vats. There was also the area below the house, known as *le rez de chaussée,* which always seemed to be in shadow. It seemed to me to have an air of mystery but was ideal for playing hide and seek when we were allowed. Later I came to realise that this was a place of refuge for father and his companions in the Resistance.

As well as memories of our family home, I have many happy memories of my grand parents' house on a hill-side just outside Cluny, in the hamlet of Brizolles. Because of its elevated position, there was a glorious panorama, (which my grandfather constantly amused himself by scanning with his binoculars), over-looking the roofs of the towers of the town. The severity of *grand-père* was equalled only by the gentleness of *grand-mère:* dressed in a long black gown, with its lacy collar and her white hair drawn back into a tight *chignon,* she was an angel of docility. The summer holidays were spent with our grand-parents there, which we regarded as paradise. We played with the other children of the hamlet and one of our games was, of course, to imagine ourselves part of the war. We made flags from branches and rags to parade through the streets and sent the boys off to the front where we girls imagined ourselves the nurses who bandaged their imaginary wounds.

Each Friday my grandmother would cycle over to the market in Cluny. In order to help her carry the weeks' provisions, my father had made her a wooden trailer. After her day at the market, she would arrive to spend the night at our house in Cluny. And then on a Saturday morning, she would set out for Brizolles with my sister and I often in tow, riding in the trailer for the flat bits of the journey, along with the week's shopping. We would sing at the tops of our voices.

It was a family tradition to celebrate each New Year all together. Our grand-parents; my uncle, Antoine Moreau, my father's brother with his wife, Germaine and their son, Serge, would join us. There were also friends such as Monsieur and Madame Hetzlen and their sons, who were refugees from northern, occupied France. On these happy occasions, my father would play his violin and sing *Ramona*; my grand-father would sing *Fields of Gold* and my sister and I would disappear under the table to giggle away out of sight.

Despite the high spirits of this New Year celebration, we soon realised that the conversation going on over our heads, which was difficult for us to follow, had become serious and disturbing. We were soon sent away to play elsewhere and not allowed to listen to their discussions. In this year of 1940, my uncle and aunt Moreau had taken a step which would determine not only their but our future history. On 18 June, 1940, they had heard the appeal of General de Gaulle, broadcast from London and in our region of Saône et Loire, they were among the first to respond. My father, convinced of de Gaulle's just cause, had also joined the Resistance. We children had no idea of the drama surrounding us and how our lives were about to be changed. Despite having always been well-loved and cared for and an outward appearance that all was well, there were indications of disturbing developments.

I suppose it began around my eighth birthday, when I became aware that we were in danger. It was a vague impression, like a passing cloud obscuring the sun or a tension in the air. My parents took to speaking in low voices on subjects which I didn't understand. One day I surprised my father when I came upon him unscrewing the base of a statue on the mantelpiece and into which he pushed a roll of papers. There were also noises, from time to time, in the room under the house which suddenly became out of bounds to us. Making some discreet enquiries one day, I came upon mattresses and blankets and signs that someone had spent the night there. All seemed worrying, mysterious and unsettling. My elder brother, now fourteen, suddenly became very self-important, regarding me as a kid who knew nothing. When I dared to raise the subject with my mother, she became very evasive but reassured me that when I was older she would tell me everything. We were at war: that I did understand.

At the end of 1942, the German army moved to occupy all of France, not only the northern zone, so we, in Cluny, were no longer part of *la zone libre*. We were now obliged to submit to an army of occupation and, despite my young age, I felt this as a sort of humiliation. A daily mistrust became our lot: everything became suspect. My great-uncle Charles and his wife, Eugénie, my grandfather's sister, became firm supporters of Marshall Pétain.

The family was now divided. Uncle Charles had fought in the first war of 1914, along with my grand-father, but now their views diverged. We no longer went to visit them. In our small town of five thousand people, everyone knew everyone else and, despite care and discretion, everyone feared being denounced by neighbours who held different views. Ancient but tenacious family quarrels were sometimes enough to push people into becoming informers. It was this which provoked the arrest by the Germans of seventy-two citizens of Cluny, fifty-one men and twenty-one women in one single day, 14th February, 1944.

14th February 1944

February 1944: I was then just ten year's old. We woke up that morning, 14th February, Saint Valentine's day, to a low, leaden sky and a bitter chill, and this morning, like every other one in winter, we would run down as quickly as possible from our chilly bed-rooms to our breakfast in the well-warmed kitchen. Each morning it was my sister and my task to take it in turns to fetch the milk from the neighbouring dairy. This morning it was my turn. Rushing down the stone steps to the pavement, milk jug in hand, I was surprised to find a helmeted German soldier, standing there, rifle on his shoulder. As soon as I stepped out, he took me forcibly by the arm and pushed me back up the stairs, shouting words I didn't understand. The door slammed shut, I flew up the stairs, terrified, to join the others in the kitchen. A glance through the window showed us it would be impossible to leave the house. German sentries in their grey-green uniforms were posted along the street as far as the cross-roads at the end. We could hear commands shouted in German, which broke the strange and heavy silence of the street. In the kitchen we spoke in low tones. Something awful was happening.

Suddenly my father was gone. He had slipped out through the cellar and across the garden after telling us to be brave and to play quietly. The morning seemed long and we knew nothing of what was happening outside. My father came back just before the mid-day meal. He had learned that a round-up was taking place and that several of his friends had been arrested. He said something to our mother in a low voice and then disappeared once more. My mother seemed sad and preoccupied. During the meal, when usually the twins, then aged three and a half, kept us laughing with their incomprehensible babbling and their funny faces, we were silent and ate hastily.

Throughout the afternoon we heard noises outside in the street but didn't stir from the house. Suddenly the sound of steps in the corridor outside the kitchen announced a visit. There was a knock, the door opened to reveal a local gendarme, whom we knew, standing there with two armed German soldiers. The gendarme asked my mother where they could find my father. Weeping, she replied that she did not know. The gendarme then translated her words into German and told my mother that she could be arrested in place of my father. We were terrified. He then ordered me to put on my out-door coat and to go and look for my father. He literally pushed me out of the door. Frightened, I began to run without knowing where I was going. Following instinct, I ran across town to the house of my Uncle Antoine, situated on the outskirts of the town, only to discover it surrounded by a group of German soldiers. Terrified now, I ran as fast as I could towards home. Arriving in the square at the end of the road, I saw a big, black car parked there. Two men in long, dark overcoats and trilby hats stood next to it. I knew that they were from the Gestapo. My father appeared, flanked on either side by German soldiers. He was pushed into the car. That image is the last I have of him. It was to be the last time I saw him.

When I returned, desolation reigned in the house. My mother sobbing, my sister and the twins huddled next to her. My older brother was not there: he was away at boarding school in the Savoy. It transpired that during my mad dash across town a friend of my father's, Monsieur Chauzy, arriving at the house in search of news, over-heard the threat to arrest my mother. He had promptly gone to my father's secret hiding place to warn him. My father then decided to give himself up. During my absence my father had returned to find the gendarme and the German soldiers waiting for him in the kitchen. Putting on his over-coat and hat, he kissed my mother, took my sister in his arms and held the two little boys tightly against him. He then followed the three men out of the house, leaving my mother inconsolable.

News of the arrests spread. Soon we heard of the arrest of my aunt Germaine Moreau, denounced for her part in the Resistance. That the Germans could arrest women provoked stupefaction. At five o'clock that morning my aunt and uncle were awakened by the screech of brakes and understood immediately what was happening, that the Germans had no doubt surrounded the town. Like us, they could not leave their house. My uncle, helped by my aunt, hid in a cavity in a thick party-wall at the bottom of their court-yard. They did not think for one moment that my aunt might be involved. My uncle stayed in his hiding place for six or eight hours without knowing was going on inside the house until his mother-in-law came to tell him that his wife had been arrested. Towards evening, the German soldiers having now left the town, my uncle departed on foot to find lodgings with sympathetic friends in the country. Three days later the Germans came back hoping to find him and arrest him. Having failed, as revenge they ransacked the house, threw the furniture through the windows and burned the lot in the courtyard outside.

When they had made all the arrests, their prisoners were taken to a square at the edge of the town, near le Pont de l'Etang and opposite the hotel, now taken over as the headquarters of the Gestapo. Here they passed the cold winter day, face to the wall, hands on their necks surveyed by their impassive German guards. Towards the end of the day they were ordered into waiting lorries and taken to the Gestapo headquarters at Lyon and from thence to Fort Montluc, also in Lyon.

In the days that followed, the families who had been left behind began to organise themselves. It was decided that a party should go to Lyon to attempt to find out what was happening to the prisoners and to take them some warm clothing and provisions. My mother and my aunt Moreau's mother therefore were among the group of people who set off to Lyon. Also among the group was the mother of my friend from school, Janine Michel. Her father had been arrested at work in his *charcuterie*. Once they arrived at Montluc, the group were allowed to leave their parcels but were not allowed entry to the prison. It also proved impossible to obtain the least indication of the fate reserved for the prisoners. At that time the entire town of Lyon was under the domination of the Gestapo and the notoriously sadistic Claus Barbie, known as the Butcher of Lyon. We learned later that the women had been taken to the holding camp at Romainville and then onto Ravensbruck in Germany while the men went to Mauthausen in Austria via the camp at Compiègne. We also learned later of the horrendous and inhuman conditions of their journeys, held without food, light or water, in cattle trucks for days on end.

My mother came back from Lyon exhausted and in despair. My grand-mother had come to help look after us:

we also had the twin's nurse-maid to help out. As the days passed, hope diminished. The wine warehouse was closed and all activity suspended. Eventually a card arrived in my father's hand-writing. It was dated 25 February 1944. It was obviously written according to a permitted formula, saying he was in good health, was with the other men of the town and asking for various items: soap, toothpaste, a note-book and pencil, a needle and some thread, some tobacco and cigarette papers. In a second separate parcel we were to send some food provisions and some sugar. It added that we were to respond in no more than forty lines and sent kisses to my mother and the five children.

This brought us some hope although huge anxiety persisted for us as my mother became more and more exhausted. At school I found it hard to concentrate. There was a small group of us whose fathers had been arrested. We didn't know why nor for how long they would be gone or where they were. At home the telephone became a sacred instrument. Each time it rang my mother would fly to answer it. Then, on March 5, 1944, a letter arrived from Compiègne, full of hope and advice:

Dear family, I am in good health. With
regard to the food here, it is not too bad
but there isn't very much of it, we are
given swede and a quarter of a loaf each
day. Fortunately the Red Cross
supplement it. I look forward to hearing

*your news, that you aren't getting too
tired since I left. Yet again I ask myself
why we are here and look forward to
being home again with my loved ones. Try
not to worry, be patient and brave as we
wait for better days.*

The message was followed by instructions for my mother regarding the management of the business.

Days, weeks, months passed. During the summer holidays we went to stay with my grandparents while the twins stayed behind with my mother and their nurse. In June, meanwhile, my uncle Antoine had returned to Cluny after being in hiding for the intervening four months. Having put his house and café back in order, after its devastation at the hands of the Germans, he decided to put it at the disposal of the Resistance workers who were anxious to regroup and so the house became the base for the Resistance Regiment of Cluny which went on to win renown in numerous combats against the Germans. My brother was back from school, and my mother, being preoccupied with the little ones allowed him to become involved: he and his young cousin, Serge, also now without a mother's care, seemed to find it all an exciting contrast to school. My mother was becoming more and more exhausted: we now learned that she was expecting another child: one who would never know his father.

In time, on July 16th a further post-card arrived this time from Germany with just a few words, meant to reassure us: *Dear family, I am in good health. Tender kisses. Claude.* These were the last words we had from him. We know now that our father was by this time detained in the camp of Mauthausen, in Austria, now, of course, annexed to Germany. We had no idea of what a concentration camp represented. As for my aunt, we had no idea that she and her companions, deported first to Ravensbruck and then to Mauthausen were being held in this camp, categorised as *Nacht und Nebel:* it was an extermination camp.

The Horror

In France the war continued. The *maquisards* continued also to defend their territory. All around our small town, bloody battles raged between the Resistance and the Nazis and we were surrounded by danger. We learned, for example, never to cross an open field in day-time but rather to skirt around the hedges to avoid German machine-gun fire. At the beginning of July there were a number of allied parachute drops bringing arms and provisions for the *maquisards*. The town was now surrounded by German troops and owed its safety to the courage of those combatants of the shadows who continued to fight off the enemy. Many were killed as a result. The German intention was to destroy the town and its inhabitants: they found it intolerable that Cluny continued to be a fierce pocket of resistance. Without the *maquis*ards of the Regiment of Cluny, it is said that our fate would have been that of Oradour-sur-Glane in the Limousin, where all the inhabitants were either burned alive (the women and children herded into the church) or machine-gunned where they stood, (the men).

At this time, the town of Creusot, fifty kilometres to the north-west of Cluny suffered horrendous Allied bombing in the attempt to destroy the Schneider armaments' factories. We were at my grand-parents on the day of the raid, and we heard the thunderous roar of the falling bombs and witnessed the sullen redness of the sky overhead, reflecting the flames below. Many Creusot citizens died in the raids, entire neighbourhoods were reduced to ruins. A short time after this we welcomed a family from the town who had lost everything in the raids and who came to live in our now unoccupied lower-ground floor. The Ayot family, parents, daughter and son-in-law became our good friends. They understood our distressing circumstances and I have fond memories of their warm presence.

In August 1944, it was the turn of Cluny to endure bombardment. The German bomber pilots were attempting to weaken or, better still, wipe out, the Cluny *maquis*ards. On the eleventh August I was in our bedroom chatting with Andrée Cuzet, the cheerful young woman who came to help us in the house. She was shaking out the sheets and bed-covers, laughing and teasing me. I went over to the window and looked out at the superb summer's day. The sky was an azure blue. Suddenly I noticed what looked like a metallic arrow flashing across in the sky. It was an airplane reflecting the brilliant sunshine and appeared to be pulling a small trailer behind it. Amused by the sight, I called Andrée over to come to see. She immediately understood that the trailer was, in fact, a stick of bombs and that we should get out of the house as quickly as possible. Grabbing me by the arm and shouting the alarm to the rest of the family we fled to the kitchen garden where we threw ourselves flat on the ground. During a brief respite we had time to run indoors to collect a few belongings: to install the twins in their push-chair and to flee as fast as possible in the direction of our grandparents' house. My mother, her pregnancy now well-advanced, found it difficult to keep up with us. Before long, another wave of bombers came over. The planes flew low, attacking the town and from where we could hear huge explosions and see billowing black clouds obscuring the sky. We stopped above the town, in an avenue, La Fouettin, bordered by ancient trees, planted originally by the Benedictine monks from the abbey. From this elevated spot we, and the other inhabitants of the town, who had joined us, fleeing in fear of being buried under their houses, could look down on what was happening. We crouched there, as the twins continued to cry, totally petrified with fear.

Those moments have left me with an impression of being caught up in a nightmare. We thought of our house, now perhaps in ruins. A bomb had fallen on the house of one of my school friends who was buried under the rubble. Many areas of the town were destroyed, the towers of the abbey and the church steeples of Saint-Marcel and Notre-Dame seeming to have served as targets for the bombers. The towers were not hit, however, although many houses surrounding them were in ruins. In the *quartier* of Notre-Dame, my great-uncle Charles' house was completely destroyed also that of the neighbours across the road from us, Monsieur and Madame Reboux. As we looked down, our over-riding imperative was to arrive as quickly as possible at our grand-parents' house and to be able to breathe in safety once more. An hour later, we arrived. Our grandparents, much relieved, welcomed us warmly. They had followed the bombing operation from their terrace, over-looking the basin of smoke and flames which was now Cluny.

After the awful shock of the bombing, we spent the rest of August at our grandparents' house while my mother, whose delivery dates was approaching, returned to the town. Our house was still standing and life continued its course. On the morning of 5 September 1944, my little brother was born at home and named Jean-Claude after his papa. The baby was very small and my mother very ill after the birth. Obviously her over-whelming and desperate anxiety state had had an effect on her health. She was unable to feed the baby herself because of a breast abscess and needed to be hospitalised. Misfortunes accumulated.

We returned to the house to prepare for the new school term. Events were so troubling that my elder brother was not able to go back to boarding school. He passed more and more time with our cousin, Serge and our uncle at the centre of the Resistance. We were now six children and my father, in the camp, was unaware of all these events. My mother, still in hospital, arranged for various helpers to come in, in turns to take care of us. We all felt a little lost. My grand-mother came often and stayed for several days, only going back to Grand-papa to organise things for him as best she could in her absence.

On the morning of October 10th 1944, my grandmother burst into the house accompanied by a young neighbour. They brought the terrible news that Jean, our older brother, had just died at the age of fifteen. He had been hit in the chest by a stray bullet whilst cleaning a machine gun. Incomprehension and amazement came before the grief. Someone must have made a mistake......I was dreaming... how could it be possible to die at fifteen? My grandmother, embracing us in tears and exhorting my sister and me to have courage, took us by the hand to take us to see our brother. He lay in my uncle's house, on a bed covered with the French flag, inert, as though sleeping. His eyes were half-closed, his hands joined together: two young soldiers stood on guard either side of him. My grandmother asked us to kiss him goodbye...

On the evening of that terrible day I stayed until my sister was fast asleep before slipping silently out of the house. Feeling as though my heart would burst if I didn't see my mother, who was still in the hospital. She would console me, she would tell me that it just couldn't have happened. At the entrance of the hospital I was allowed in, despite the lateness of the hour. The ward was silent and shadowy as I reached my mother's bed-side. As I approached, I saw my mother weeping silently. I took her hand without saying anything. She opened her eyes, seemingly un-astonished at my presence and said simply "How are we going to tell papa when he comes home?"

Life continued. My mother came home at last from hospital and our daily life recommenced despite the sadness. The stifled sobs of my mother, now dressed all in black, accompanied our days and our nights. We no longer sang. My violin stayed in its case and my sister didn't go near the piano. From now on music was no longer part of our life. People reminded me gently but persistently that I was now the oldest and must set a good example and shoulder my responsibilities. It was a heavy burden for a child of ten to shoulder still over-whelmed with grief. Each Sunday our walk had now one objective: the cemetery. It was a torture. My mother was in black from head to foot, pushing the baby's pram, with the twins trotting behind and my sister and I bringing up the rear. During the walk our neighbours spoke consoling words to us but which only served to increase our misery.

At Christmas 1944 we had a happy surprise. The friends of my late brother Jean, boys of fifteen or so, came to the house to deliver a magnificent Christmas tree which they had decorated with garlands, candles and baubles. They had commissioned a carpenter to make dolls' furniture for my sister and me: there were wooden toys for the twins and a rattle for the baby. This kind gesture gave us a true moment of happiness.

The winter months passed without us knowing anything of the fate of my father. At the beginning of 1945, the Allied advances had given us hope that we would soon see an end of the hostilities and that our father would come home. We had to wait, however, until 8 May 1945 for the end of the war. I was in class that day when suddenly all the bells of the town began to ring. The headmistress summoned us all to the play-ground to announce that 'The war is over!' A wave of joy over-whelmed me. I can see myself now, sitting on the steps thinking of my father's return, and that life would continue as before. The memories of moments shared with my father that I had guarded deep in my heart surged into my mind like no-longer-hidden treasures...the day he had accompanied me for my first day at school ... I felt again my hand in his and I longed to feel again that sense of warm protection. It was not to be.

The first American tanks arrived in an atmosphere of celebration. The soldiers lifted us in their arms, thinking, probably, of their own children back at home. They brought us chocolates and sweets made with real sugar and of which we had forgotten the taste. We also discovered chewing gum for the first time. All the world seemed to be celebrating and we began to look forward to seeing Papa once more. A long period of waiting now began. The radio announced the liberation of all the camps by the Allies. Then on 13 May 1945 I made my first communion. Despite my beautiful white dress it was, for me, a day of unhappiness and also rebellion. I was very angry with God for sending us so much sadness. For my companions it was a fete-day with their families. In our house, however, there was no joy, for there was no question of celebrating without Papa. I was losing hope and my faith faltered. We were beginning to get glimpses of the first arrivals from the camps. Slowly they came, stepping out of the lorries, near-skeletons with haggard eyes, in striped pyjamas and seeming to come from hell itself. The stories they had to tell were so incredible that they soon began to feel that people did not believe them and so they refused to speak of what they had lived through. The convoys continued but my father was not among them. We listened as the radio gave the lists of the deportees repatriated to different countries. We lived close to the telephone by night and day. One moment of joy over-whelmed us when we heard the name of my father along with that of the mayor of Cluny, also deported, liberated by the Russians and sent towards Odessa before being moved on to France. The waiting seemed interminable. But the news proved to be an administrative error: this wasn't a rare occurrence where, with such confusion reigning everywhere, announcements turned out to be wrong. My father's companions, now returned, confirmed our worst fears, that we would not see him again. My aunt came back and our cousin, Serge, mad with happiness, was reunited with his mother. His Christmas wish of 1944 had been granted. Asked by his father what he would like as a present for Christmas he had written on a tiny piece of paper, found much later, 'I would like a return ticket for my mother'. As for my grandfather, he could never admit that his son had disappeared. Until his death thirteen years later in 1958 he always guarded the hope of seeing him again.

My father was reported as 'disappeared' officially on the 12 April 1945, eight days before the liberation of the camp. For others in Cluny, however, there were the celebrations: the cries of joy, the military parades, the award-giving ceremonies, the posthumous medals. It was explained to the orphaned children that they must be proud of their father's sacrifices: they were asked to carry the huge wreaths of flowers at the head of the official delegations and parades. The widowed mothers stood, in tears, their hats wreathed in black veils. It was a strange consolation to receive a cross attached to a ribbon in a velvet case. I wanted to scream "Keep your cross and give me my father!" But it was necessary to give the impression of being honoured by the presentation. My grief was so strong, however, it left no room for other sentiments. Pride did come later, when I eventually understood the part my father had played in that insane war. But at that time, in

1945 my head was filled with clashing, turbulent sentiments: pain, indignation, anger, incomprehension. Despite the passing of the years, that wound has never healed.

During the years when I was bringing up my own family I had a sense of remorse at not having had the courage to look into the past and especially the circumstances surrounding the disappearance of my father. Little by little we had learned what the Nazi concentration system entailed. As a result of discussions with the former deportees, we had learned the awful details of their detention. It was difficult to ask them questions for fear of causing further hurt. I learned much from my Aunt Germaine who is one of the few remaining witnesses of those terrible years. Her deportation to Ravensbruck, then to Mauthausen did not succeed in destroying her or making her embittered. Over the years we learned more as books came to be written. Then my sister and I had the opportunity to take a course at the Memorial Foundation for the Deportation where we were both enlightened and overcome. Our personal quest, however, must rest without an answer. No-one could deliver us from the anguish when we thought of the truly dreadful end of our father's life, presumed to be 12 April 1945, just a few days before the camp was liberated by the Americans.

It seems that now it is impossible to be ignorant of the horror of that period. It seems also that we have a duty to transmit the truth to future generations. The monstrous genocide of the Jews will be forever inscribed in memory. The men and women of the French Resistance; the political prisoners, hostages, victims of reprisal attacks are many: they too had to suffer the atrocities of the camps, because they opposed the invader and defended their country. The ashes of those brave people who did not return will be forever mixed with the earth of Germany, Austria, Poland and even France. The children orphaned as a result of that war have also paid the price of suffering at the hands of the Nazis. My thoughts go to my Cluny friends, the orphans of St Valentine's Day 1944 and to others too numerous, who must never be forgotten. They are now, for the most part, grandparents and who remember all too well the traumas of their childhood. They must witness in their turn to that which must not be denied and must watch that the world does not forget. One of the reasons for writing this account was to make sure this story is transmitted to future generations.

Today, more than half a century after those childhood years, my memories remain intact. I have discovered in playing with my grand-children feelings of happiness and joy which were stolen or forbidden during the years of my childhood. My grand-children will remember, I hope, that great-grandfather whose ashes were dispersed somewhere in Austria on the banks of the Danube in a camp of extermination, sacrificed with so many others for their beliefs and their desire to live in a free country. They are an inestimable gift to their descendants. These pages are a homage to his memory.

Chapter Ten

The Belot Family

Author's note:Father of four, André Belot, then aged forty, was arrested on the 14th February 1944 along with three other employees at the Cluny gas works. They had taken responsibility for the radio transmitters hidden there which were used for relaying messages to and from the Allies. At that time he and his wife were expecting their fifth child. This was Guy (the author of the second account below), who was born 6 weeks after his father's arrest. He is now a handsome, white haired man in his sixties and it was he who was central to the work of collecting and publishing the Cluny testimonies, only a handful of which are translated here. He also organised the exhibition which accompanied the book. He was Cluny's deputy mayor for some years. Jeanine, his older sister, the author of the first testimony below, married a student from the College of Arts et Métiers, Monsieur Camille Georges. All three still live in Cluny and play an active part in the commemoration of the deportees.

Jeanine Georges (née Belot)

This is the story of that small girl of eight years' old who witnessed the events of that awful day, 14th February 1944. I was at home with my mother, one of my brothers and my little sister. I had my nose stuck to the window of the family apartment at 11 Prud'hon Street, Cluny. My older brother, Jean, 19, worked with Monsieur Janin in St Mayeul street as a gardener: he also lodged there which was the reason he wasn't at home with us that day.

It was cold and miserable that day in Cluny, it had snowed and turned to sludge. Very early that morning there were lots of comings and goings of cars and lorries, of sudden shouts in German voices and the strident shrieks of whistles: all this comes back to me. We had not been allowed to go to school that morning, because we had been forbidden to go beyond our street. Then I saw a lorry came along with people sitting in the back. Among them we saw our father. Our looks crossed through the window, he appeared overwhelmed and very sad. I only have to close my eyes today to feel the emotions of that moment again. I was too young then to understand what was happening. He had been arrested at the gas works, along with his boss Georges Malère.

In the afternoon, I saw my mother leave for the Hotel Chanuet, (the German headquarters in the town) where all the people arrested during the morning were being held. She was seven and a half months pregnant and hoped therefore that the Germans might show some pity, but it was no good. She had hoped too to be able to see our father and give him some warm clothing. She came back to the house with the parcel. She had not been allowed to see our father again.

…………………..

After that awful day we received very little news, apart from a couple of post-cards. My mother managed as best she could and six weeks later gave birth to my brother Guy on 29th March. As she had five children to feed she didn't hesitate to take on whatever jobs she could to earn some money. She cleaned people's houses, took in washing and carried on working in my father's vegetable garden. I remember her often setting off on her bicycle for her home village of Buffières, returning with some food for us: we never went hungry. We bigger children looked after the little ones while mother went out to work. She never gave in and although there was never anything much left over when all was done and this is what worried her most. It was a hard existence for us all and if the *Restos du Coeur* (1) had existed then we would have been able to benefit from them.

Three months after my father was arrested and taken away, my maternal grandmother died which was yet another blow for my mother.

．．．．．．．．．．．．．．．．．．．．．．

After the bombing raid of August 11th 1944 (2), for us as for many of the Cluny folk, there followed a very difficult period when we had to leave our home and move away to the country on account of all the buildings which had been damaged or destroyed. The alert had been given during the morning that there was to be a German bombing raid. All the family went into the garden to find a hiding place, camouflaged, we hoped, among the bean poles. Once the first bombing raid was over we left for La Cras. Mother would have preferred to go back to her own village, Buffières, but she was obliged to follow official recommendations. During the afternoon while on our way, we were shot at by German aerial machine gun fire. We tried to find shelter behind the field hedges and stone walls to avoid being seen: this wasn't easy for mother with five small children. Mother was reprimanded by the others when the wheels on Guy's pram caught the sun's rays – they were afraid we'd all be spotted by the German 'planes. Brother Henry had the task of getting the pram over the hedges and other obstacles. Mother had Guy in her arms and I looked after my little sister, Danielle who was nearly three.

We were at La Cras for eight days, staying with various families (Madame Rambaud, Madame Brun and others…). After that we stayed in a small house belonging to Monsieur and Madame Gelin before finding our aunt and cousin Bérard along with some other families at an ancient spinning mill at Merzé where we stayed for about three weeks.(3) We were then told that it was possible for us to go home, the streets having been cleared of rubble and debris from the bombing. Our street, Prud-hon Street had been well and truly devastated. Guy, now nearly five months old and little Danielle came back beautifully brown from our enforced stay in the country.

………………..

Months passed, with their share of sadness and problems. In the spring of 1945 the deportees began to return, which brought mother more distress when she saw the state they were in and how they had changed: ill, skeletally thin, grey haired…and no news of father whom she hoped would be among them. Then came the final shock: someone came to tell us that father had died on 25th August 1944. Having seen the state of the people who had returned, mother would well imagine the fate of our dear father. We learned little about how he died. Monsieur Jaillet, the jeweller, told mother that he had seen him ill with typhus. We would have liked so much to know more, but no-one dared talk of what they had lived through.

Mother managed to keep going and carried on working to raise her family with dignity. She was working as a paid daily help, notably for Madame Burdin who came back much weakened after her months in the camp and needed a lot of help. I think they were mutually helpful to each other and I have a huge amount of respect and affection for Madame Burdin. Mother knew little about financial assistance but the town council's Benefits Office awarded us four kilos of bread a week from Monsieur Jaffre's bread shop in our street. We were also allowed free medical treatment. Later on, mother, who was considered a war widow, was awarded a modest military pension as well as a reversion pension (4): this was only minimal, however, as Father had only worked at the gas works for seven years.

Our precarious family situation did not, unfortunately, allow us to undertake long years of study or to do what we might have wished, career-wise. The local person in charge of the 'National Pupil Scheme'(5) suggested I learn sewing as a boarder at a school in Charolles while I had dreamed of becoming a school teacher!

As time passed, we all became very proud of our mother who helped us, by her example, to make a success of our lives despite the absence of our dear father, so much missed by us, over the years. I think in particular of my younger brother Guy who never knew him. As my grandson, Matthew, aged eight, said to me "Granny, you were lucky to know your daddy for eight and a half years but Uncle Guy didn't know him at all".

In 1979, during the Easter holidays, my son (aged 16), my husband and myself went to Mauthausen and to Gusen. It was as a sad but necessary on pilgrimage for us. We placed a plaque in memory of our father at the Memorial behind the cremation ovens at Gusen where he died. We went back with my sister, Danielle and my brothers in 1994: united in intense emotion. To see once more the place where my dear father gave his life for his country has helped me find some degree of peace of mind.

Guy Belot: a wound which will never heal
Warm inside my mother's womb on that cold Monday morning of February 14th, I waited 43 days before I opened

my eyes to this world, to be born into our modest apartment at number 11 Rue Prud'hon. I can imagine the tender looks and smiles of those surrounding my mother, my two brothers and two sisters, as they leaned over my cradle, forgetting for a moment the continuing drama which had, by then, been going on for nearly two months. In fact the happy event was over-shadowed by the anguish at my father's absence after his arrest at work as part of the huge round-up in Cluny. That had been organised, of course, by the Gestapo following denunciation by those in Cluny who remained devoted to the Vichy government and their regime.

For my father and for the other inhabitants arrested during the operation, it was, one after the other, first the cellars of the Military Hospital in Lyon, then the jail at Montluc and finally, in France, the camp at Compiègne. From here, correspondence had been possible and so my father knew about the birth of his son. One can imagine the heart break of this man, brutally separated from his wife and five children. Probably he saw himself back home before long, but he had no idea of the hell of Mauthausen-Gusen that was ahead of him and that he would die there, on 25th August 1944 in atrocious conditions. For my father and I destiny was already sealed: we would never know each other.

In place of that irreplaceable contact I have only a photograph, a fragile evocation but so very precious to me. This picture, attached to the wall of my bedroom, allowed me to establish, over the years, a monologue when I wanted to talk to him which, little by little, transformed itself into a special dialogue where I could imagine his answers to my questions. How many years must pass before I knew what happened to him and to accept the reason why I didn't have a father like the other children? It is difficult to explain the disappearance of someone he has never known, to a child, when, in addition, there is no possibility of explaining the death of that person who is now just a name at the foot of on a tomb stone.

In the conversation between children the question "What does your father do?" came up often. "He died after deportation." That didn't satisfy the curiosity of the questioner but I couldn't add anything else and often they didn't ask. I have to say that we hardly spoke of it at home. My mother spent all her time working in order to raise her five children, to show us her love and protection. Sure - when the grown-ups talked about the war and all that - I listened very carefully but without being able to join in: that was the rule in those days: children were seen but not heard.

Despite all, however, my brothers and sister and I grew up with our memories. Since 1948, when the monument to the deportees was erected at the Pont de l'Etang, near the square where they spent their last day in Cluny, I don't think I have missed a single commemoration of that unforgettable day. Each year it was the one occasion where we were allowed to miss a morning's school so that we might attend the ceremony. It began with Mass at the church of Notre-Dame and from there a procession began, with the flag at its head, and wound its way to the monument where the official ceremony took place. In the afternoon we went to school. Looking back, it seems that the masters, at least the ones who taught our age-group hadn't taken the trouble to discover what was being commemorated. Perhaps they feared re-opening old wounds and causing more heartache. Yet they seemed to have an intense desire to know:

"Dead for France? What does that mean?"
"Mauthausen? Where's that? What did
they do?

We always faced the same silence on the subject. No exhibition: nothing written: no discussion in the schools about it. The truth had to be discovered piecemeal: here and there, in snatches of conversation.

It wasn't until I was in my teens that I began to slowly discover the purpose, the magnitude and the horrors of the Nazi camps: the gas chambers, the crematoriums, the striped prison uniform, the dehumanisation, the suffering, the organised deaths and the sacrifices made by men and women, martyrs for their country. It was then that I began to understand the annual ceremony of remembrance at Cluny and knew why I found myself there, before that monument with all the names engraved in stone: Benoît

Alix, Gustave Arpin, François Baury, Jean-Baptiste Beaufort, André Belot … It brought back to me memories from early childhood. I understood the reasons why mother told us firmly that we were not to greet such or such a person whom we met in passing during our Sunday afternoon walks. "They did us too much harm", she would say. She spoke of notorious collaborators who dared parade with impunity. She had surprised one of these sinister individuals in the act of listening outside the door in the corridor of our apartment. What more could that swine B have learned from us? My father had already been taken and my mother had five children to look after! Such cowardly behaviour illustrates the climate of denunciation that existed during that time.

I also realised why I was at the inaugural ceremony on August 15th 1948 with my mother. Although I was only four, I have never forgotten the memory of General de Lattre de Tassigny pinning the Croix de Guerre on the chest of the war widows lined up before the monument. When he drew level with us he tapped my on the cheek with a paternal gesture. Did he say anything? If so, what? I will never know for certain. But for the memories to have stayed with me so clearly, I must have been much impressed by his stature, his brilliant uniform and the military music. No doubt the child that I was remained indifferent and impatient as the speeches of Doctor Pleindoux, then Mayor of Cluny and François Mitterand, then Minister for the Forces and Victims of War. I knew, later, the reason why a delegation from the police, including an officer from Mâcon came to our home to present my mother with the Légion d'Honneur and the medal of the Resistance awarded posthumously to my father. It was a simple ceremony, full of emotion. But there again, I was probably more impressed by the decorations and the uniforms of the officers than by any sense of what it represented.

I remember that one Christmas I was given some second-hand toys. My mother said to me "It's a Mauthausen Christmas." I will always remember the green wooden lorry and a toy farm. Like all children I played with the 'Mauthausen lorry'. Later I came to understand that these presents, from which I had benefitted, came from the collections organised by the 'Friends of the Deportees of Mauthausen' and were distributed to the orphans of the dead deportees of that dreadful camp.

Over the years, I understood why my mother had been obliged to work as hard as she did. Her war widow's pension, (which she did not begin to receive until 1948) was less than the minimum wage of that time was not sufficient to support her family. That was why, as well as working as a domestic she did the laundry for the families she worked for so that there was always an odour of soda crystals throughout the house. Then, through all weathers, she would load up her hand-cart with enormous piles of washing in order to take them to be rinsed in the *lavoir* down by the river. On Thursdays, during the school holidays I would go with her, playing where she could keep an eye on me. I do not think I will ever succeed to fully appreciate all she did for us: she raised us without ever asking anything from anyone.

The evocation of all these memories didn't solve the mystery of what happened to the father I so wanted to have known. What sort of father would he have been for me? How would we have got on? I had never talked about things like this with my mother: we were very close and neither wanted to risk causing pain to the other. I only knew that he loved children and that he never scolded my brothers and sisters. Only my sister, Jeannine could talk to me about him. My two older brothers had left home and Danielle was only two and a half when my father died.

On 9th August 2004, Madame Germaine Moreau came to talk to us about the Resistance and the deportation. She told me that she had known my father. Her words went straight to my heart and my tears began to fall: the least detail had the effect of bringing comfort. To say that one had waited sixty years before talking of these things!

In 1971, for the first time, we went to Mauthausen. Our anguish grew as we drew towards the end of the 1,000 kilometres journey. Near the village, we discovered the imposing and gloomy granite fortress, surrounded by ground upon which grew only suffering and where the only harvest was death. We walked around the camp: it is impossible to describe our feelings: the 186 steps to the quarry: the gas chambers: the torture rooms…. We went into the cells, covered with hundreds of inscriptions, signatures, often scratched into the plaster by finger nails and, of course, we searched for our father's name.

In the camp museum we wanted to see all we could, to read it all, to check everything we could. A window! Inside an open register! And suddenly a shock! At the bottom of the page was the name of my father: André Belot Fr. 59551 (the number we knew), born 4-12-1904. We were able to translate 'Saint-André-le-Désert', his birth place. The right hand column was undecipherable to us but the left hand column noted the date of his death: 25-08-44. Once we had recovered from the shock, we realized that we had experienced the unimaginable: to find in that book, held by the executioners of the camp, the name of my father among all the 300,000 (of whom 120,000 died) who had known this cursed place of misery and horror. The sadness remained but, at last, we were in possession of a document: a photocopy of that page which we brought back to Cluny in our suitcase.

In 1994, after my mother's death, we went back as a family to Mauthausen. The register was there, as before. The page confirms that my father shared in the communal life with 300,000 others, stripped of all humanity and that he died 25th August 1944. Some questions, however, can never be answered about how he died: was he able to confide in one of his companions? Did he have a friend to help him through his last moment on earth? The only hope that we try to hang onto is that he was already dead when his body was taken to the crematorium. The account of the death of George Morlevat, with whom my father was arrested on 14th February 1944, suggest that was not always the case.

One would wish to believe that it is a question of a nightmare from which one will wake up happy to see the day but…the worst is that it is all true.

Chapter Eleven

The Gendarme's Story: The Pautet Family

Author's note: Claudius Pautet was born 30 kilometres north-west of Cluny in February 1900. He spent his working life in the Gendarmerie Nationale, until he retired in 1952 as Assistant Chief Officer at Cluny. Unlike Britain, in France there are three different police forces (1). In Cluny in 1940 the Gendarmerie, with its courtyard and big wrought-iron gates, resembled a military barracks in the centre of the town. The gendarmes lived within the barracks in individual apartments. Claudius, his wife and two sons, Louis Robert and Guy, lived in one of these apartments. Their story is told first by Claudius's wife, Marie Pautet and then by his two sons.

Louis Robert's account also describes his own young experiences during the war years and also of his witnessing the important battle of Cluny on 11th August 1944. (The Germans were intent on destroying Cluny as a centre of the resistance. It is described in full in chapter 13).

Guy's memoir recalls the family visit, after his father's death, to the camp where he was imprisoned.

September 1943

My husband, the warrant officer (second in command) at the Cluny *Gendarmerie* was the second person to be deported. On 13th September Claudius Mangeard had been arrested and then on 29th two Gestapo agents, in their trilby hats and black raincoats, called to speak to him at the *Gendarmerie* As he wasn't there they left a message with his colleagues making it clear that he must attend the *Feldgendarmerie* at Mâcon the following day.

He went as requested but after he had gone to talk to his chief in Mâcon. He told my husband that, knowing of the arrest, he had asked the German authorities to telephone him after my husband had been interviewed. As no phone call was forthcoming, he went to the German headquarters to find out what was happening. He then saw my husband, who was handcuffed, but was unable to speak to him. He rang me that evening to warn me that Claudius would not be coming home that evening. He came in person the following day to Cluny to give me more information. On the evening of September 30th, I learned that my husband was imprisoned in Fort Montluc at Lyon. I received only one postcard during his time there although I was able to learn more from Monsieur Lambert who had also spent some time in that same prison.

In the following February, 1944, a few days after the round-up at Cluny on the 14th, Claudius was in the prison courtyard where he spotted a group of Cluny people, among them the station master Monsieur Arpin and also Marie-Louis Zimberlin, the school mistress. Mlle Zimberlin managed to pass a note to him, hidden in a piece of bread, using as an intermediary a woman whose husband was employed doing maintenance work at the fort. The message indicated that all was well at home and that we

154

were all in good health. From that, my husband gathered that something unusual had taken place in Cluny.

In due course, on February 24th, he was taken to Compiègne with the others from Cluny. He was given the role of cell leader and shared his cell with Father Riquet; Aldebert, the designer, and the former minister, Christian Pinault. I received a parcel from the camp containing his personal belongings and also four religious medals given to him by Father Riquet. Throughout his time in captivity, my husband kept a fifth medal which, he said, had brought him solace. I received two post cards during his time at Compiègne: one on February 25th and one on March 8th. Sometime after that, on 22nd March, he left with others from Cluny for Mauthausen where he arrived on 25th March.

My husband was always very reserved about his activities with the Resistance. It was only after his death that I found his personal papers, which showed he had been a member of the Free French *(Forces Françaises Libres)* from the 1st March 1943, with the rank of Sub-Lieutenant. My son Robert and I have just finished reading *Chiens Maudits* by Georges Loustaunau-Lacau (2). We discovered through reading my husband's notes that he followed the same route as the author throughout his time in Mauthausen. Under the chapter entitled 'The Cattle Truck' my husband had written: *"I was in that wagon."* The chapter reads as follows: *After being searched, the prisoners were marched to the station at Compiègne: we*

were made to climb into cattle trucks, a hundred at a time.
Later, following several attempted escapes, the order was
given that all prisoners should dismount and undress. We
then had to get back on the train, this time with two
hundred per wagon, but in their birthday suits. That
journey lasted three days. The many prisoners who tried to
escape were shot by the German soldiers accompanying
the convoy. Others perished after atrocious suffering,
without food or drink, suffocated inside the cattle trucks.
Arriving at the camp at Wiener-Neudorf, our reception
lacked any ambiguity: "Work! And don't forget that we
have the power as to whether you live or die!

Cluny, February 14th 1944

At around five o'clock that morning German soldiers
arrived at the metal gates of the *Gendarmerie* barracks and
rang the bell. The duty orderly was told to summon all the
staff. Whilst visiting each apartment to wake the sleeping
gendarmes he was accompanied by two German soldiers.
The *gendarmes* were then requisitioned to lead the soldiers
into the town where they were to indicate the homes of the
people whom they wished to question. They had copies of
the list of names. The *gendarmes* wives and children were
confined to the building until around 1.30pm. Two German
soldiers guarded the gates. I was, however, allowed to go to
do the shopping. My older son had tried to leave to go to
school but was sent back by the guards. He was no sooner
inside than he slipped out through the kitchen window on

the side of the building. He only got as far as St Odile's gate before he was sent back again, this time passing the two sentries who let him in without question.

The people arrested were taken to *La Place de l'Etang*. Thinking that the *gendarmes* would be obliged to follow the prisoner's convoy to Mâcon, they sent messages back to the wives at the *Gendarmerie* asking them to bring them their overnight things, some clothes and toiletries. However, they weren't required to accompany the convoy and were back in barracks by five o'clock. Those they had arrested were taken to Lyon to the School of Military Medicine. The following day, the Germans came back at five am and, accompanied by the *Gendarmes,* continued their arrests. We learned that Mlle Zimberlin (3), the school teacher, had been arrested.

The Return

My husband came back on the 7th May 1945, the day before the Armistice, after an absence of 19 months. The Commander of the *Gendarmerie* at Mâcon let me know that morning that my husband was at Annemasse, (near Geneva) and that he'd be arriving in Cluny around four o'clock. The meeting place was fixed in the square, near the Chanuet Hotel (the same place from which the prisoners had left) on the edge of the town on the Mâcon road. Accompanied by my three children we set off in one of the *gendarmerie* cars to meet him. The Cluny *gendarmes* accompanied us on their bicycles decked out with little

French flags. We saw the cars from the Mâcon brigade pull up 30 metres away.

My husband got out of the first car accompanied by the Commander and the Captain. It was a moment of great emotion. He stood looking at us for a minute or so walking towards us. How we valued that moment, followed by many embraces! All four of us had within our minds a picture of a man in good physical health, more than six feet in height and weighing more than thirteen stone, we had before us a frail-looking man of seven stone. His eyes gleamed with happiness, however and I could tell that he was refraining from allowing emotion to overwhelm him. He also seemed as though he wanted to apologise for his lamentable state of health - a visible testament to his suffering. What a totally unforgettable moment!

It had been planned that we should go on parade around the town preceded by the Cluny *Gendarmes*. Given my husband's state of health, however, the procession passed just as far as *La rue Prud'hon, la place du Commerce* and *La rue de la Liberté* before arriving at the *Gendarmerie*. When we arrived a photograph was taken in the courtyard to mark the occasion.

Son Louis-Robert tells his story

In June 1944, along with my friend René Bourgeois, (both of us were students at Cluny Technical College), I joined the French Forces of the Interior. They had the responsibility of organising the *maquis* at Cluny. As we were too young to participate in any actual fighting, we were taken on to do other useful jobs.

In October 1942 there had been a number of Allied parachute drops. These were meant to provide the *Maquis* with arms (Sten machine guns, grenades, explosives) and with the means of communication (transmitting / receiving sets). There were also 'sweeteners' - cigarettes, chocolates etc. Up until 6th June 1944 the parachute drops had all taken place at night under a full moon. After the Allied landings however, the 'planes came in by day, guided on the ground by the *maquis*. People still remember the drops of the 14th July at *La Grange Sercié*. It was around mid-day that 36 Liberator bombers escorted by 50 fighter planes arrived, bringing in more than a hundred tons of armaments. The message sent from London announcing the imminent arrivals had spread like wild-fire around the town: "Arriving tomorrow with 36 friends".

All the equipment came in metal containers attached to the parachutes: some parachutes failed to open and so the goods inside were smashed on hitting the ground. It was our job to take the damaged equipment back to the College to examine it and, if possible, carry out any necessary repairs. We did this, good engineers as we were, under the watchful eye of one of our foremen, Monsieur Barraud. After having disposed of the arms that were irreparable, we proceeded according to two principles: one was to straighten the barrel of the Sten guns: the other was to remove any intact parts of any arms totally irreparable so that they might be used elsewhere. After that we had to make sure the repaired arms were fit for purpose. To do this we were required to fire a magazine at a pumpkin in the garden behind the workshops – precision wasn't considered important! The school also had stocks of deteriorated stuff like Camel cigarettes which gave off an odour of honey. But this stock was kept...

Knowing that the German army was still in Mâcon, 25 kilometres from Cluny, weren't we aware of the danger? Since 6th June we were under the impression that the town had been liberated and the active members of the Resistance moved around the town quite freely and without fear. The population, we thought were completely behind the cause. Yet skirmishes between the *Maquis* and the German army became more and more frequent. On the 2nd July during the battle of Azé several young men of the town had been killed. I remember the death of one friend, Lenfant, aged 17... A large crowd gathered at the cemetery for his burial in the presence of a delegation made up of members of the Resistance. There was no thought that the enemy might not be very far away.

From time to time I went out to the hamlet of Corcelle, about 7 kilometres from Cluny, to buy farm produce from Monsieur Lapalus. It was a few days before the 11th August 1944 and this time M. Lapalus was surprised to see me arrive, coming as usual along the route between Bourgvilain and Tramayes. as, he said, mines had been laid on the entry to Bourgvilain. On the way home, being careful but curious and thus getting off my bike, I walked along the lower side of the road. I could see a dozen or so small metal bosses along the middle of the tarmac, announcing the presence of explosives. I got back on my bike once I was sure I was out of danger!

Author's note: in this next section Louis describes his experiences during the battle for Cluny on August 11th 1944. A full account of the battle can be found in chapter 13.

During the night of 10th – 11th August we were told that a German convoy was coming in the direction of Cluny. That morning, about 7 o'clock, I was hoeing a row of carrots in our allotment there. I realised there was some sort of battle going on at *Le Col de Bois Clair,* the pass just beyond Cluny on the Mâcon road. It didn't surprise me as virtually every week the German convoys travelling towards Mâcon were attacked there by the Resistance. Towards half past eight, I stopped for a sandwich. As I sat I saw, coming towards Cluny from the south, three airplanes in formation. I wasn't able, at that distance, to identify them. They circled the town, turning to the east to then come back over from the south, one behind the other at an altitude of 400–500 metres. When it was over the builder's merchant's factory on the southern edge of the town, the first 'plane dived towards the ground as a black shape detached itself from underneath the 'plane. For a moment I thought perhaps it was one of the Allied aircraft dropping leaflets: it was possible because a month earlier, on July 14th, we'd had a big parachute drop in the middle of the day. The two other 'planes continued on their trajectory.

I soon lost sight of the black shape but a few seconds later I heard a huge explosion. Turning round I could see the mass of black smoke rising above the town: then I understood that it was the German air force coming to bomb the town. The missile seemed to have fallen in the market square. I was aware that there was a battle going on at the *col de Bois Clair* and I concluded that the German infantry had called for support from their air force. I ran towards two men who were gardening at the far end of the allotment telling them to get indoors. They were surprised as they hadn't heard a thing! The other two 'planes came back from the south, following the same trajectory, releasing their bombs one after the other. Then the three 'planes turned back towards their base, machine gunning the Resistance positions at *Bois Claire* on the Mâcon road as they left.

It was the first time I had witnessed a bombardment. I distinctly saw the three bombs leave the 'planes. After the first, not having any idea what was happening, I didn't feel any apprehension. The other two, however, passed directly over my head and I was afraid that one of them might get me…happily they fell about 300 metres away. I went home as fast as I could to reassure my worried mother.

At the beginning of the afternoon I went back into Cluny to see what damage had been caused by the bombardment and to offer my services to those responsible for co-ordinating the work. They were busy clearing the Abbey Hotel in the central square and the Simonot's wool shop where there were several dead. We were at work there when, at around 5.30pm the siren went and an airplane passed over our heads again at an altitude of 400 – 500 metres. Immediately we were told to stop work and go home. I ran to re-join my family, never losing sight of the tiny airplane which continued to turn above the town, machine gunning and releasing sticks of bombs over the buildings, the surrounding fields, the streets and main routes. People were trying to flee but were in fact providing further targets for the machine gunners. I soon realised – and other witnesses have confirmed it – that the missiles were not hitting their human targets: clumsy firing or an attempt to spare the civilians? My friend, René Bourgeois, who got out of the town at this point along with a hundred or so others, all fleeing north towards Salornay-sur-Guye, saw the machine gunner shoot at his neighbours. But the bullets didn't touch them and fell a good fifty metres away. Other planes, perhaps the ones which came during the morning, bombed the lower, St Marcel district of the town.

I came back towards the end of the day to help carry on clearing the rubble. The town was practically deserted the majority of the population had gone to find refuge with friends or family in the surrounding countryside. Going down *Rue Prud'hon* I came upon M. Jaffre, the baker, still working calmly away in his bakery. Seeing my astonishment at his presence he responded calmly "My poor Robert, I was at Verdun in the '14–'18!" Looking at the destruction in Rue Prud'hon, La Place du Commerce, the market square, all around the church of Notre-Dame, I felt very bitter. What a desolate sight! What a tragic day!

During dinner that evening, M. Lefeuve a retired army captain, came to ask us if we could accommodate him and his family for the night in one of the barns. My mother offered to provide beds for them in the house. Feeling very happy with this offer, he left to find his wife, his young son and his elderly mother whom he brought along in a wheelbarrow! We had heard nothing, during the day of what had happened out at *Bois Clair* but, that evening, having had news of the situation, M. Lefeuve advised my mother that it might be wise to keep the children up with some provisions at the ready so that in case of danger she could leave the house for the woods with me and his young son. This reassured my mother.

The morning after, we learned that the Germans had fallen back as far as Mâcon and had lost both men and equipment. I went back into Cluny and in passing in front of the hospital, saw that an uncovered lorry was stationed. There were a group of men there taking out the bodies of the *Maquisards* killed during the fighting of the previous day and loading them onto the back of the lorry. It was the first time I had seen a dead body; I was overcome by the thought that these young people had given their lives for us, the people of Cluny.

In the streets, however, there was great animation provoked by the presence of all the *maquisards* who had participated in the German defeat. It was the last time we saw any Germans in the vicinity: there were no more after 12th August. The Resistance took on the responsibility of ensuring the security of the town properties in the absence of many of the townsfolk. There were identity checks put in place on entry to the town and I helped keep the guard for several nights in the Notre-Dame area, where bombing had been severe and many properties damaged. The townsfolk came back slowly. The majority of them found the houses and their belongings intact but for many others there were many difficulties which would need their urgent attention. Cluny now faced major problems with regard to reconstruction which would make profound changes to the appearance of the town. The Allies finally arrived in Cluny on 4th September 1944.

Guy Pautet, Son: A Pilgrimage

My father had travelled to Hell and beyond. Sixty years later, in July 2004, my brother, Michel, our wives and my son, underwent a journey of remembrance to the Mauthausen camp. Like so many of the deportees, it was only rarely that my father could find the words to talk about his ordeal during that year. However his body continued to express the traumas inflicted on him and the other prisoners: deprivation and torture left its evidence on those who came back from the camps. It was on coming back to Cluny in February 2004, coming to see the exhibition mounted in honour of the deportees, that we finally decided to execute a project which I'd thought about for a long time – to go to those same places where my father had endured so much unspeakable suffering during those fourteen months.

And so on Sunday 11th July 2004 at nine o'clock, we crossed the mythic Danube, which that day wore a suitably sombre aspect. We walked the few hundred metres through the typical Austrian village, with its multi-coloured houses with their ornate carvings. It was in passing one of these abundantly coloured houses that I felt a strong and deeply personal shock. Before me, as if torn from the pages of Epinal was a carved and painted image, about three metres by two. It was an illustration of a dentist, exercising his art in a manner neither dignified or worthy. All the ingredients of the scene were aimed at highlighting the cruelty and barbarous nature of that profession. In other circumstances that satire would almost certainly have made me smile, as it was my own profession, but here in Mauthausen, where my father had met with almost daily barbarism, I lost any sense of amusement and remained troubled by that coincidence.

After a visit to the village it was with some difficulty that we found directions to the camp, indicated by a small unobtrusive notice "K.Z Mauthausen 4 km". It was as though it was presenting excuses for its presence. This reminded me of one of the inhabitants of the village who said in an article in the newspaper "When we go on holiday we never say that we are from Mauthausen".

The Camp appeared suddenly before us with a field of cereals beyond, as we'd seen on photographs taken in 1945. All was before us: the surrounding wall, the surrounding watch towers, the chimneys from the cremation ovens, the roofs of the barracks. Our emotions, already heightened would mount throughout the visit reaching a crescendo in the infirmary transformed into a museum.

Having read and re-read so many books and testimonies concerning the camp, I could imagine my father in every part of the camp, in the showers, exchanging his civilian clothes for the striped 'uniform'; in the parade ground, frozen, standing there in all weathers; in the infirmary for his damaged foot; in the evenings in the overcrowded huts as the deportees took their rest, waking to the ranting of the sadistic Kapos, bringing them back to an awful reality…or perhaps down below the camp, down the steps of that renowned staircase to the quarry of death or, more exactly to hell with whichever comrades who had been judged fit to break up those granite blocks to the point of exhaustion or beyond.

Few words were exchanged during that visit: throats were too dry. There was instead the thought that the pictures we had seen in books on Mauthausen were now replaced by the reality of this place with a dramatic intensity. My mother, my brothers Pierre and Robert, in fact all the family, preserve deep feelings of homage to my father after his long and terrible ordeal in this awful place (4).

Chapter Twelve

A Nurse's Story: Marie Angély Rebillard

Author's note: Marie Rebillard celebrated her ninetieth birthday in 2012. She was a trainee nurse at the outbreak of war and worked tirelessly with the Cluny doctor Dr Pleindoux throughout the war, caring for Resistance fighters as well as civilians injured during the August 1944 bombing raids. After the war she trained as a social worker and spent her long life working with the less fortunate in Cluny. A devout Christian, she recently gave her family home in central Cluny to the town, to be used as a research centre for scholars who wished to come to study the history of the abbey. A well-known and well-loved figure in the town, she was the first person I met when beginning the research for this book. She then introduced me to the people whose stories I have told in this book. Despite her years she continues to live an active life in the town. This is her story.

On the 14th February 1944, a little before seven o'clock in the morning, mother and I left home, at 18 Station Avenue (now known as Avenue Charles de Gaulle) for St Marcel's church where a memorial service was to take place in memory of my maternal grandfather who had died a month earlier on 11th January. We had not gone far when we came upon two German sentries, standing outside Monsieur Nigay's hotel-café-restaurant.(1) One of them came towards us, pushing us back saying "You must go home." Mother insisted and showing him the prayer book she held in her hand said "Church, church" but it was no use "Raus! Raus!" We had no choice but to obey.

Aware that something unusual was happening, once home I went up to my room to put on my nurse's uniform. Shortly afterwards, an open lorry drove down the road, the sort used by the highways department: it had around ten people sitting inside it. It stopped and Monsieur Nigay, accompanied by the German sentries, was made to get in. I can still see him, in my mind's eye, seated at the back, wearing his fur-lined jacket.

Learning a little later that the milk had not been delivered to the hospital and knowing that the Maternity unit was running short, I attempted to get to the Duroussey's farm, intending from there to carry on to the Hotel Chanut (the German headquarters) to see if I could be of any help to the people who had been taken away, perhaps taking them some item of clothing or taking a message to their families. There was no way of knowing what might happen to them. However, before reaching the gasworks I was forced to retrace my steps. We knew nothing more until that afternoon. Suddenly we heard a huge noise. From the windows we saw that all the furniture from Monsieur Nigay's café-restaurant was being thrown out of first floor windows, smashed to pieces and fed to a huge fire now blazing in the middle of the near-by square.

That really opened my eyes to the necessity to do something.

It was not long after this that my friend Mademoiselle de la Moussaye came to ask if I would help organise a small rural hospital for the injured men of the *maquis*. I accepted without hesitation. Our first visit was to Bourgvilain, a small village seven kilometres from Cluny to the home of the Favre family (an elderly mother and two single daughters, Jeanne and Marguerite). Our request that they shelter the injured men was quickly accepted but Mlle de la Moussaye made them understand the dangers, should the Germans discover what was going on there. They all responded to us with unanimous pride that the men were risking their lives and that it was now the turn of women to do the same.

We began by making arrangements to have an old building in some near-by woods repaired, so as to be able to evacuate the wounded if that were necessary, and we got together the equipment necessary to organise both bathrooms and an operating theatre. If these plans proved impracticable, the Favre household was able to accommodate some convalescents from the military hospital (which had been set up in the College of Arts and Technology buildings at Cluny). It operated from August until the end of October 1944 and received some fifty or so men. I was also able, under the auspices of the Red Cross, to work alongside Dr Pleindoux and Sister Chabert in

Cluny in giving First Aid Training and we managed to train twenty to thirty people.

....

In 1944, worried about how elderly people living alone without family living near-by were managing to find food, we started off a support service with the help of the local Scouts. A list of people willing to help was drawn up with the help of Monsieur Lanquetin. We divided Cluny into areas with five or six people in each to be visited each week by a volunteer, a girl who came from a good background with political opinions we could rely on. In each of the surrounding villages someone was then delegated each week, to buy eggs and if possible cheese, so that we could get fresh farm produce to these elderly folk, who were unable to get about either because they lacked any means of communication or local contacts. Everyone helped, no-one refused. Sometimes goods were donated, which allowed us to distribute products at prices which could beat all competition. The understanding and the generosity of everyone meant we were able ensure some nourishment for these elderly people and also firewood (cut down in the woods belonging to the Count de Milly-Lamartine), as well as all the wood from the demolition of the damaged buildings after the bombing of Cluny in August 1944.

One could say that all the town helped with the activities of our elderly support service: the students from the Arts and Technology College helped cut the wood; the stables at the Stud Farm (2) provided the harnesses and equipment for the carts; teams of men from the town did any clearing up and provided any house-hold improvements needed; teams of women weighed out the goods, parcelled them up and prepared the baskets for the 'visitors'. They came each week, on an agreed day to pick up the orders at the permanent office set up in la Place de la Liberté. Then, when school was finished, the children carried the baskets to the elderly persons in their street. As for supplying the town with vegetables, deliveries weren't at all regular and information was circulated at the last moment, by word of mouth if the town crier was not available.(3) Elderly people often didn't get to hear him or they arrived too late because they couldn't walk very fast, or else they had difficulty in standing in the interminable queues and had little chance of being served. We also duplicated by means of a Roneo machine a small monthly bulletin to keep people informed of news: deaths, marriages, advice, bits of useful information of all sorts.

11th August 1944

At Marly, Mlle de la Moussaye had hidden the weapons belonging to the 5th Dragoons and also hidden several officers of the Secret Army (4). I had heard one of them say that Cluny was going to be bombed. Sworn to secrecy, impossible to talk about it to anyone, I wondered what was to be done about evacuating the elderly who were sometimes lodged high up in rooms at the top of the tall town houses. That gave me a constant cause for worry.

During the first bombing raid on the morning of 11th August however, it was impossible for mother and I to do anything other than run and lie flat in the vegetable garden. After it was over I wanted to get to Bourgvilain in my nurses' uniform, in order to help, but it was impossible, there was fighting at Ste-Cécile. I went instead to Cluny (civilian) hospital where the injured civilians were arriving, their numbers increasing all the time as a result of a second wave of bombing. Most of the townsfolk had fled, taking refuge in the surrounding countryside while the more able-bodied and courageous among them were getting on with searching through the rubble. Among our team of First Aiders, only Jean Bourdon, the hairdresser, had come to the hospital to help. Night had fallen when we heard that Sister Isabelle, one of the Sisters from the near-by convent had died. She had been brought to the hospital earlier, along with another injured Sister as a result of the convent chapel targeted by machine-gun fire.(5) The mortuary was already full and the corridors full of the injured lying on stretchers while the doctors were busy in the operating theatre. We needed her bed and so had needed to take her body back to the convent.

Thus, Jean Bourdon and myself set off up *la rue de Ravattes* with the deceased sister on a stretcher. With Jean in front and with me behind, taking care where we trod with electricity and telephone cables strewn all over the ground, we were fearful of falling with the body. Eventually we arrived at the great door of the convent: it was difficult to open it as the sisters were all in the shelter and out of ear-shot. We could hear the German planes circling overhead. Finally we were able to find somewhere to lay Sister Isabelle to rest. Jean, without more ado, rolled up the stretcher, put it over his shoulder and set off as fast as he could whereas I, groping my way in the dark among the fallen electricity cables, managed to follow la rue de Ravattes and get back to the hospital. Once back I was ordered to take charge of the maternity ward for the night and without a midwife! The emotions undergone by the mothers as a result of the bombing had brought the time of their delivery nearer.

Some days afterwards, at the end of the afternoon, the sisters at the hospital told me that three military gentlemen had arrived in the chapel of the main hospital and wished to talk to me. I thus found myself face to face with Major Mazué, physician and future mayor of Montceau-les-Mines; Major Laurent Bazot and a third I did not know but I later guessed to be Captain Chadru with whom I was to work. He was a surgeon and also chief medical officer at the newly-established military hospital, temporarily installed in the College of Arts and Technology. Major Mazué spoke to me: "Mademoiselle, you have chosen to give your services to the injured members of the Resistance, we must tell you that there are seven of them in the military hospital". I asked what he wished me to do and was told he would like me to accompany them to the military hospital in order to help there. I thus had to tell Matron that I could not continue to work at the civilian hospital. This did not please her at all!

I could tell a long story about our arrival that first evening when the team was gathered: ambulance men (with a gas-powered van that was not always willing to start and was a real headache for our mechanics), drivers, medical students, surgeons etc. At first I was the only nurse to have been recruited and was given the title 'Nurse-Superintendent'. Soon, the arrival of Mlle de la Moussaye and Monsieur Garnier (from the Mâcon Red Cross) allowed me to complete the nursing team needed to care for the vast dormitory. That first evening I quickly established what was most urgent: getting hold of bowls in order to wash the bed-ridden; pillows to provide an extra layer over the hard mattresses (a number of our patients had received back injuries). So I organised a collection of equipment from the surrounding houses: several of the women I called on offered to come and help cover the night-duty period.

Although the military hospital was only in operation for a limited period (August, September, October, 1944), our time together there created a real *camaraderie*. Although most of the group are no longer alive, I always have great joy in meeting to share memories with Captain Chedru, who, despite his great age and long medical career also has warm memories of that short period.

1945

After such a long and anxious wait, the return of the Cluny deportees was a moment of great emotion for both the families and the townsfolk who came out to welcome them. I was particularly struck by the frail condition of Madame Burdin and Monsieur Jean Alix, both neighbours from the far end of the town.

Shortly afterwards I was asked by Dr Pleindoux, the town doctor, to help with his examinations of the returned prisoners. These took place at the hospital at Cluny and we were given the operating theatre for our use. I remember that Dr Pleindoux, in conducting these examinations always apologised for not being able to be more discreet, and the responses of the women were along the lines of "You cannot imagine the manner in which we have been treated: everyone in front of everyone else in the showers, in the assemblies – completely nude."

I also remember that, given the task of taking the medical reports to Mâcon, to the military doctor there, I was struck by the casual manner in which I was received by him: he was sitting on a table, swinging his legs and smoking a pipe - this officer to whom I must give the reports did not alter his position, (as one might have expected) not just because of the young girl that I was at that time but out of respect for the accumulation of suffering contained in those files. I had received terrible secrets in confidence and this man who was responsible for receiving the trains arriving from the camps accommodated everyone in a mixed centre, no doubt having no idea of the dramas that could ensue with all-comers accommodated in the same place.

My experience of Cluny during the war subsequently played a significant part in my decision to stay in Cluny and follow and accept a senior post in Social Services at the Headquarters of the Health Service. I had had to interrupt my studies at the College of Nursing and Social Services at Lyon when my father died and I didn't now feel sufficiently experienced or qualified to take on the care of 24 rural communes. However, it seemed to me that with a common sense and some feeling for others I should nevertheless be able to manage it. And so it was that on 1st June 1945 I set out on the adventure with Social Services that marked my life for 42 years.

Chapter Thirteen:

The Battle for Cluny: 11th August 1944

Author's note: This next chapter is markedly different in style from earlier chapters, which are, of necessity personal and subjective, their being the memoirs of the people and their children who lived through these years. This chapter, in contrast, has largely been translated from the work of military historians, some of whom fought there on 11th August 1944. (1) It has its place here, however, for the battle for Cluny was critical in the history of the town. There is evidence that the German intention was to obliterate the town, its Resistance forces and townsfolk alike as had happened at Oradour-sur-Glane (see Chapter 9 and note7 below). After the Allied landings in June 1944 and given the strength of the local Resistance the town considered itself liberated. The Germans, however would not allow this state of affairs to remain unchallenged.

By the summer of 1944, Cluny was regarded as the capital of the Resistance in the Saône et Loire region, partly as a result of its strategic position at the intersection of major trunk routes and also as a result of the local groups of *maquisards* who were well-organised, dispersed and mobile. Cluny had become the headquarters of the regional Resistance. The command structure based there controlled the deployment of forces, finance and rations distribution. It also took responsibility for the support of the fighters' families. There was a feeling of determination and control, tangible throughout the town. The willing participation of the public services, the police, post office and the local authority made a unified Resistance organisation possible.

Since the Allied troops had landed in Normandy on 6th June, Cluny like many other towns in France, wisely or unwisely in some cases, considered itself liberated. The young men of the *maquis,* armed and bronzed, circulated freely in the town meeting no opposition. Their cars had been adapted for fighting with rear windows removed. Lorries moved freely around, packed with men and military equipment. A feeling of euphoria reigned. This close co-operation had not come into being overnight. The town first welcomed STO 'refusers' *(refractaires)* at the end of 1942 and by 1943 the local groups of the *maquis* were in place in the surrounding woods and hills. 1943 also saw the first reactions of the occupying forces to this growing centre of resistance, leading to the round up and deportation of nearly 100 people in February 1944. Following the shock of these arrests, the *maquis*, nevertheless regrouped and continued its activities, harassing the German troops, intercepting their convoys and sabotaging their communications.

After the D-Day landings, there was a combined regional force of 8 units. In Cluny and its environs, a proper military structure was now in place, organised into sections, companies and battalions.(3) These were made up of the *maquis* and the *sedentaires,* (those who had continued their civilian life whilst trained and ready for combat when needed) (2). They were led by a number of former French army officers and SOE agents. The troops numbered in all between 2,000 and 2,500. The current absence of patrolling enemy air cover or German garrisons in the immediate vicinity meant that daylight parachute drops were feasible. On 14th July and again on 1st August 72 bombers of the US Air Force brought over 100 tons of armaments: 900 containers inside which were 2,376 items of arms and explosives.

The three local Resistance sections for whom these supplies were intended were Charolles, Cluny and Saint-Gengoux-le-National (five miles to the north-west of Cluny). These sections were led by three senior officers: English Flight Lieutenant Albert James Browne-Bartoli (pseudonym 'Toto' or 'Tiburce') who was head of the SOE Dichter network; Canadian Guy d'Artois and a French captain, Jean Régnier. These all worked under the command of Georges de La Ferté, (alias Férand), the Chief of the French Secret Army (4). Following the long-awaited Allied landings in Normandy, their immediate task was to delay, harass and, if possible, to prevent the German forces from moving towards the north to reinforce their troops engaged in the battle of Normandy. It was therefore of the utmost importance to arm, train and equip the *maquis* for sabotaging and attacking these German convoys on the major trunk roads and railways.

Following instructions from the SOE HQ in London the team were to ensure that a triangle of terrain, with Cluny at its centre and bordered by Mâcon – Paray-le-Monial and Chagny (just south of Beaune) was kept as far as possible free from enemy incursions. The SOE considered the area ideal as it was relatively easy to supply, there were well-established resistance networks and everyone knew everyone else which made for safety from any fifth columnists.

Cluny is 22 kilometres to the west of the main Paris-Lyon-Marseille road and rail axis. The base of the triangle was formed by the RN79, Mâcon – Charolles. The rail line from Bordeaux to Strasbourg was on its eastern flank, as was the route to the north-west via Bourges and Orleans to Normandy and the advancing Allied Armies. If its strategic importance had not escaped the notice of the local leaders of the SOE, the German Commanders of the forces garrisoned at Mâcon were also well aware of it. Despite their repeated engagements against the *maquis* they had enjoyed little success in reducing resistance activity. Among their by now limited resources there was a battalion of the Freiwilligen-Stamm-Division.(5)

Two historical factors may have some bearing on the events which followed and on the further rousing of German ire. On the 20th July there had been an unsuccessful attempt on Hitler's life and secondly the Allies under General Patton had broken out of the Normandy Cotentin peninsula and were beyond Avranches by 1st August. Not only did this require major German reinforcements but the exit routes back to Germany, should the situation continue to worsen, were also threatened. Since D-Day the local resistance had made frequent guerrilla attacks on German convoys, being increasingly better armed, equipped and trained, thanks to the SOE-organised parachute drops and the agents in the field. The Germans therefore made a strategic decision to attack Cluny in order to destroy the centre of the Resistance support system. By this time, the Germans had neither sufficient time nor resources to destroy piecemeal concentrations of *résistants*.

The combined regional *maquis* were armed with sub-machine guns, with a few heavier machine guns, mortars and explosives. They were well-organised and well-led, in particular by Laurent Bazot a former regular French officer (6). The Germans were far more numerous, well-armed with artillery of various calibres and could call upon aerial support. They were led by SS officers and the troops were for the most part of eastern European and Mongol extraction, veterans of many atrocities against the civil population on the eastern front and latterly had arrived in Mâcon after taking part in the massacres at Vercors and Oradour-sur-Glane *(7)*. They were therefore used for carrying out savage reprisals against civilian populations and were not specialist combat troops. They were not expecting to meet well-organised or well-armed resistance fighters.

In order to protect the town, a number of *maquis* units from the neighbouring villages were put in place to the north and to the west of the town while units from Cluny itself took control of the south and eastern approaches. This was the route most likely to be taken by the German troops stationed at Mâcon, 25 kilometres away. Cluny was separated from Mâcon (where the German troops were stationed) by the valley of the river Saône and also by a line of high wooded hills. This made it highly defensible. There were a number of narrow passes (known as *cols)* which dominated the high ground along the N 79, between Mâcon and Cluny. These allowed early observation of approaching enemy units. There were also courageous agents in place, one of them a telephone operator in Mâcon who were able to give advance warning of the approach and strength of German troops. There were road blocks and observation posts along the approach roads from the north and west and thus Cluny was relatively well protected. There had been an earlier skirmish on the 2nd July where the Germans had experienced the power of the *maquis* in restricting their movements and attacking their columns.

On August 10[th,] the *maquis* were warned by a clandestine telephone call that a German column was due to leave Mâcon at 21.00 that evening. From 23.00 onwards, various *Maquis* patrols sighted the German column and confirmed that Cluny was their probable destination. They mobilised to defend the town. Their problem, however, was how to know which direction the Germans would take. There were three possible approach routes. They surmised that the *Col du Bois Clair* (the narrow pass through the wooded hills to the south of Cluny on the N79 Mâcon road) was probably the most likely route and therefore needed to be held. They placed other units across the approach from the N80 coming from the south-west and set up machine gun emplacements along the other main route into Cluny, past Berzé le Chatel. Interestingly, the castle there had been built in the Middle Ages to defend the Abbey of Cluny.

None of these preparations turned out to be in vain. The Germans in fact used a three-pronged attack, coming, as they thought, to deal swiftly with lightly-armed and disorganised 'terrorists'. The main thrust was through the pass, the *Col du Bois Clair*. The *maquis* engaged the German forces around 04:00, fighting a courageous battle against a formidable opponent. Not expecting such heavy resistance, the Germans summoned aerial support which arrived in the form of three bombers, which attacked Cluny around 07:00. This did little to dent the effectiveness of the *maquis*, who were fighting a critical battle some distance south of the town: it possibly increased their resolve. The Germans finally managed to break through the pass by 10:00. The *maquis* fell back to the line of the river Grosne and were reinforced by other companies coming from the north-west.

This delay of the German attack plan turned out to be highly significant. It had given the *maquis* on the southeast of the town time to prepare an ambush on the route past Berzé-le-Chatel including fifteen heavy machine gun emplacements. They allowed the German column supporting their right flank to proceed along the route to Cluny until it was all within range of the guns. The *maquis* opened fire with devastating effect, virtually annihilating the entire German unit in twenty minutes. This was followed immediately by Laurent Bazot ordering a strong counter-attack against the main German forces across the River Grosne and by 16:00 the Germans had been forced back beyond the cross-roads of the two main axis routes of RN79 and 80.

The Germans then called in a second wave of aerial support which bombed the town around 17:00. By this time most of the townsfolk had fled to neighbouring villages and the town was almost deserted except for *maquis* reserves and about two hundred people sheltering in the cellars. The town doctor, Dr Pleindoux and Red Cross nurses, including 22 year old Marie-Angély Rebillard, continued to care for the injured and dying civilians, as well as the returning *maquis* casualties. All in all, 28 buildings were destroyed and 14 civilians killed, including a nun who was helping care for the wounded.

Having lost their right flank, the Germans had withdrawn by 20:00 and did not renew the attack. The *maquis* continued to harass the route of the N6, beside the

River Saône, which runs north-east from Mâcon: the Germans however had neither the time nor the means to attack Cluny again, given that the Allies landed on the southern coast of France, on August 15th. (See note 9, chapter 14).

The outcome of this battle in terms of casualties was 10 men lost by the *maquis* and 53 wounded with 8 prisoners taken. On the other hand the number of Germans killed in this engagement was 170. Had the resistance not been victorious, it is highly likely that Cluny would have suffered a similar fate to other towns and villages which were destroyed and their civilian population massacred in the most brutal way, as at Oradour. The Germans did not attempt any further incursions into the area, resigned as they now were to defeat. With Cluny now truly liberated, the Resistance forces were free to assist in the liberation of other towns in the region. Mâcon was liberated on 4th September where they were able to welcome the regular French forces who had landed in Provence three weeks earlier.

Chapter Fourteen

Liberation

The first half of 1944 was one of the most violent periods of the war throughout southern France. By the spring of that year, much of southern, rural France could be more appropriately described as 'Resistance France' rather than 'Vichy France' as in many areas the Resistance was having more impact on people's lives than the Vichy government. *Enfeebled from above by the Germans, from within by the collaborationists, from below from the Resistance and from outside from de Gaulle, the Vichy government existed only in a nominal sense. (1)* As the regime lost control, however, it became more violent and unpredictable. The strong man was now Darnand (2) and the French police were required to work directly with the Germans. Darnand however, believing the French police were no longer reliable, resorted more and more to the French militia. The new director of prisons, Jocelyn Marat, for example, was a *milicien* who dressed as a Nazi and gave the Nazi salute.(3) After Pétain's broadcast of 28 April 1944 condemning resistance terrorism, the militia became even more unrestrained. Darnand's organisation was now attracting increasingly marginal, even criminal elements of society. *In its last stages Vichy has been described as a fascist regime (...).The regime had become a police state – or milice state – which existed only to crush its enemies (...). The regime lived on fear. The executant of this policy was*

Darnand; its orchestrator was Philippe Henriot, the French Goebbels. (4)

After the Allied invasions of June 1944, the German troops retreated north to support troops fighting in Normandy. Hence they found themselves in areas previously unknown to them and where no contacts had been established. Local commanders who believed they had established a *modus vivendi* with the local French population (although this was not the case around Cluny with its strongly active Resistance) were furious when the brutality of the newly arrived troops destroyed such relations. Troops from the SS Panzer *Das Reich* division, many of whom had spent the last three years fighting on the Eastern Front, were responsible for some of the worst atrocities as at Tulle and Oradour sur Glane as they moved up through the country. (5,6). There is no doubt that without the actions of the local Resistance forces, Cluny would have suffered the same fate at the hands of this division, who were more used to carrying out savage reprisals against civilian populations than fighting well-organised and equipped fighters such as they met at Cluny on 11th August.

....

When the Allies finally landed in Normandy on 6th June 1944 the French Forces of the Interior (FFI), which now included all the Resistance fighters, were ready to play their part. They harassed the German troops as they moved north, destroyed railway lines, intercepted their convoys and sabotaged their communications. The Germans were now under no illusion that the Resistance, along with its young *maquis* members, were a genuine military threat in the eventuality of a landing. In accordance with the Allies' wishes, the French intelligence service (*The Bureau Central de Renseignements et d'Action)* had issued an 'Instruction on the military action of the French Resistance' which was communicated to the FFI regional commanders in March 1944. This anticipated a three-stage battle: the coastal region (five days), the bridgehead (four to six weeks) and finally the liberation of the rest of the country (four to six months). The Resistance would be provided with specific objectives: preventing the movements of German reinforcements to the coast (Tortoise Plan), sabotaging rail transport (Green Plan), disrupting radio communications (Violet Plan), and targeting electricity lines (Blue Plan). But it was emphasised that there should be no insurrection. (7)

Churchill had at last been convinced of the role the Resistance could play in the coming Allied invasions. In and around Cluny, the Local SOE agent, Captain Albert Brown-Bartoli (Tiburce or 'Toto'), who headed up the 'Ditcher' Resistance network along with his American radio-operator, Joseph Litalien, (known as 'Tintin') ensured that the area was well equipped. Red, white and blue parachutes came sailing down in broad daylight on 14th July (8), bringing over a hundred tons of armaments and explosives in thirty six Flying Fortresses. There were further 'deliveries' on August 2nd and 31st. The Cluny

Resistance forces were being prepared for their part in the battle for the liberation of France.

Liberation assumed many forms and was, in fact, a series of liberations as towns across the land gradually declared themselves free. Now that the local Resistance had control over the major routes of the area and also of the town, Cluny had declared itself liberated, rather earlier, perhaps, than was wise. It was an understandable reaction after so much suffering over the past four years but it also served as a provocation to the German forces. As a result there had been a series of violent battles before the official liberation by the Allies, on 4th September:

- 8th June: the Germans attack at the *Col de Bois Clair* on the Mâcon road – 2 FFI killed
- 10th June: the arrest and disappearance of Jean Renaud, a revered member of the resistance and instrumental in its instigation in 1940
- 15th June: German attack at the *Col du Loup* : two FFI and one unknown person killed
- 2nd July: Battle of Azé: 18 FFI killed including 7 young *maquisards* from Cluny
- 11th August: The Battle of Cluny: the final defeat of the enemy and the end of offensives against the Resistance. 20 FFI killed, 50 injured: considerably more losses on the German side. The civilian population lost 14 victims under the bombardment with many buildings destroyed.

- 4th September: arrival of Free French Army. The Cluny Regiment went on to participate alongside in the liberation of Mâcon, Sennecy-le-Grand and Chalon. From then on, for those who wished to go on fighting, the regiment was integrated into the First Army of General de Lattre.

Personal Experiences of the last days

There now follow some personal stories giving us first-hand accounts of those final days of the war in France. The first is the testimony of Maurice Ducrot. He joined the maquis after having refused the summons for the obligatory work service (STO) in Germany) in 1942. He recounts the arrest and disappearance of Jean Renaud, his friend and an emblematic figure to the Cluny Resistance Regiment, he being the initial instigator and right-hand-man of 'Tiburce', the local SOE agent.

....

Maurice Ducrot: On 10th June 1044 morale was high, knowing the Allies had landed. We lads from the *maquis* were out and about in the town. Five or six of us had lunch together in the square and then went down to the station to pick up some supplies, sugar, flour etc. for the chaps out at Crue. We also distributed supplies in the town to those in need. Suddenly, as we approached, a chap warned us "Be careful, the Germans are here!" A train carrying German troops had just arrived at the station and the Boche were getting off, guns at the ready. They were no doubt intent on carrying out reprisals. Jean Renaud, brave as ever, said, "Come on, let's go and see what they are going to do". He then proposed that we go for a beer in the station buffet. I wasn't too happy with the idea. But anyway, we were waiting to be served when six Germans rushed in, their rifles fifty centimetres from our noses. They were looking for Jean Renaud. He'd been pointed out to them by the train driver (who was condemned by the Court of Justice at Chalon after the war). We had not suspected him of being a collaborator.

I'd been warned not to allow myself to be taken alive. On the quiet I'd got my hand on my gun. If I was going to get it, they'd get it as well. I could see that Jean was eyeing the possibility of escaping. All of a sudden he made a dash towards the door leading up to the first floor. The Boche leapt after him, shouting. As for me, I took the opportunity to get myself out of the door on the other side which led into the square. I'd managed to reach the foot of the steps outside when Jean leapt from the upper window, nearly hitting me but falling instead flat on his back on the steps. He was at my feet and couldn't get up. He was asking me to pick him up while the Germans were yelling "Stop, Stop!"

The train's arrival meant a lot of comings and goings and general confusion. This meant that some of the lads had been able to get away. Could I? Could we – the two of us – escape? Taking advantage of the confusion I got myself into the middle of the crowd leaving the station.

A car was parked just across the road, outside the hotel. It was one of the ones we had pinched from the Germans. Those cars had given us loads of trouble – two hours to get them started – but this time – a miracle – it started first time. I jumped in and set off in the direction of La Chaume to find Lucien, our *Maquis* chief. Rochat arrived at the same time – he'd heard what had gone on at the station.

As for Jean Renaud, we never knew what happened to him. Claude Rochat (pseudonym Commandant Guillaume) has written that he was killed in Cluny. That isn't true. The next day with Father Dion we set out for Chalon on our bikes to see if we could find out more of what had happened to him. But at the station there no-one knew anything: he hadn't got off the train or been taken off. We went everywhere to try and find out, apart from the prison. We would never know what happened to him.

....

Another young *Maquisard* at the time, Henri Gandrez writes:

If I had to keep just one image from my time in the Resistance it would be the memory of those young patriots of the Cluny *maquis* who died at the Battle of Azé. My brother, Robert Gandrez, who was 20 and acted as a liaison agent was taken prisoner, tortured by the Gestapo at Mâcon and shot on the 6th July 1944 at Varennes-les-Mâcon. Raymond Jeanniard, 20, also died there. Robert Lenfant, who was well named as he died a hero at just 16. Badly wounded during the battle he died in the hospital in Cluny.

I was with him as was our commander, Laurent Bazot, who was holding his hand. Before breathing his last he said "My Captain I am going to die but tell me that I haven't died for nothing and that we are going to win the war". These were last words of a young French patriot.

....

Another young member of the Resistance was Michel Burdin whose mother, Madame Suzanne Burdin, was deported to Ravensbruck for helping supply food to the *Maquis* up in the woods. He writes:

Finally the 6th June 1944, the day of the Allied landings arrived. I remember so well the code message sent from London. Despite the usual interference we heard the words *Jeannot lapin met des culottes de satin* (Jean Rabbit is putting on silk panties) which signalled the landings were imminent. What joy! What relief! Using pins, we began to plot the progress of the Allied troops on a map of France. In Cluny, because the *maquis* were so strong and the Germans came near us only rarely, we already had the impression that we were liberated. We were going to be soon disillusioned, however when they tried to destroy the town on 11th August. However they didn't succeed!

Chapter Fifteen

Return and Aftermath

The Return

No matter how great the wave of euphoria and joy which swept France after the Liberation, the uncertainty as to the fate of the deportees tarnished any such celebrations. This was nowhere more so than in Cluny, where families waited anxiously for loved ones to return. Nothing had been heard of them since they left the transit camps at Romainville or Compiègne Were they alive or dead? It was going to be a further eight months before the uncertainty ended. When, however, the first survivors returned, it was obvious to all who saw them that there would be some who would not be returning.

For Michel Burdin the dreadful 'adventure' of that awful 14th February "ended at last for my mother, when she came home during the night of 29–30th March 1945. The joy of having found her again was tempered by the realisation that there were those who would not be returning. My mother's physical state was a witness to what she and the others had suffered. It required a long period of convalescence and a period at a rest home in Chambéry for her to regain her strength. On the 8th May 1945 the Germans unconditionally surrendered. My father and I were on the way to Lyon when we heard the news. We immediately turned back to find the town already celebrating. We set up a public address system in the market square where it seemed that everyone from Cluny and the surrounding villages came to dance every evening for a week! The Fair came and set itself up and stayed for two months during which we recovered some of our *joie de vivre*. Our family was once again back together. We now had to re-learn how to live as a family and get our business going again. As for me I went back to my studies at the Technical College but, as a result of a stupid accident, I had to give it up and start work in the family business. Over the intervening years we have never talked about that period of our lives. The subject appeared to be taboo. It seemed better to draw a line under all that had happened. I dared not ask the questions that sometimes seemed to burn on my lips until the day that my mother was able to tell us, by means of her writing, of her life as a deportee. The events of those days profoundly affected me at that young age and in many ways determined my future path in life as it did for so many others". (1)

From February 1945 until early 1946, and especially in April and May 1945, the thousands of French civilians who had been deported to Germany were returning home. The arrivals from the Labour camps caused considerable shock. Most people had little idea of conditions in the German concentration camps. Many assumed that the deported Resistance fighters would have lived in conditions akin to those of prisoners of war. We have already heard the voices of those who returned and of those who welcomed them home: the shock and horror when they first saw the condition they were in: skeletal and in rags. Some 97 people from Cluny and its surrounding villages had been sent to the camps, 21 of them were women. Of the 97 who went off, 49 died in the camps and did not return, 2 of them were women. Madame Suzanne Burdin, deported to Ravensbruck who returned home in April 1945 wondered why the deported women seemed to fare, in terms of survival, better than the men. Was it a combination of circumstances, being subject to less demanding labour; being able to withstand privation more easily, or was it the sense of mutual support they offered each other, the small tasks they were able to carry out to make their lives less horrendous? Certainly a strong sense of unity existed among them, continuing as they did, after the war, to meet weekly to support each other.

Most of the returners, however, were young men at the beginning of their adult lives who, once recovered sufficiently, wanted above all to resume a normal existence and not talk about the horrors they had witnessed and experienced. How could they make the people back home begin to understand circumstances far beyond anything they could have imagined? Some of them inevitably found it difficult to fit back into French society. In many cases their health, both physical and mental was badly damaged with effects which continued with them for the rest of their lives. Eventually they did begin to want to talk. But it took until the 1980's when these people, now for the greater part retired, began to want to explain their war-time lives to their grandchildren and to future generations. It was when these often self-published memoirs began to appear that it became clear how far both the deportees and also their children, the succeeding generation, had been affected by these war-time experiences. There were also the orphaned children of those deportees who wanted to ensure what they and their parents had endured was not forgotten.

Memories

What memories did people retain of war-time France after 1945? Memories of World War One had been unifying, on the whole. Every French village and town has a war memorial listing huge numbers of dead. In contrast there are few such village centre memorials of World War Two. There are, in fact, many, but they are scattered across the countryside, in fields, on mountain tops and in woods, showing where a *maquisard* or a Resistance fighter fell, where hostages were taken, where battles were fought, won or lost. Each area, town and village will have experienced the war differently and will have different memories. Memories could be divisive as well, for decades after the war French people could still point out, around the village or down the main street, where *'collabos'* had lived. Post-liberation, de Gaulle worked tirelessly to ensure national unity and thus the over-riding myth was of the glorious resistance of the nation. It was the late 60's and early 70's before the process of untangling myth and reality began.

Marcel Ophul's film, *Le Chagrin et Le Pitié* (The Sorrow and the Pity) of 1971 was considered 'one of the most important documentaries ever made'. (2) Made for television and not passed by the censors for broadcasting until 1981, as it was considered too iconoclastic. (3)

Post-Liberation

De Gaulle's desire for national unity meant that many former figures of the Vichy regime were tolerated and, after a while collaborators were pardoned. Pétain, however, faced trial and had his death sentence commuted to life imprisonment. Laval was shot. Some 100,000 people were condemned to penalties ranging from loss of civil rights to death, although less than 800 were executed. By this time, however, there had been an uncontrolled unofficial purge of '*collabos*' – "by Resistance fighters shooting members of the *milice*, local groups lynching apparent traitors and shearing the heads of women who had slept with German soldiers or simply individuals for personal reasons taking revenge. It was not pretty". (4) This period, known as the *Epuration Sauvage* (Wild Cleansing) preceded the setting up of the special Liberation courts in early September 1945, allowing the civil and legal authorities to take over and the courts to be set up.(5) It is difficult to know how many died during that period, numbers vary according to whom you read: evidence of the confusion of the immediate post-liberation period. The approximate number of people executed before and after the Liberation was approximately 10,500, including those killed in the *Epuration Sauvage*.(6)

At this time the Resistance worked in two directions: one continued the fighting where necessary, the other was putting into immediate position people who knew how to run railways, post offices, the *Gendarmerie* etc.(7) Cluny had its own *Comité Locale de la Résistance* (CLR) until it gave way on 14th August to the *Comité Départmental de la Résistance* (CDR) whose role was to ensure that administration and services ran smoothly, thus replacing Vichy-led organisations. They also had the task of 'unmasking' the collaborators and *miliciens.* This led to 27 arrests in Cluny. These people were held in *le Farinier des moines,* (the monks' flour mill, one of the Abbey's out-buildings), which was used as a provisional detention centre until the civic authorities and Courts of Justice were in place to try them. There exists a copy of a letter written by 19 Cluny women to the President of the newly-restored Republic asking if their accused husbands could be released from their make-shift prison to await judgement.

The Resistance also had its own form of unofficial *Epuration Sauvage.* During the war they had their own ways of letting partisans of Pétain and Hitler know that they were being watched. They might find a swastika painted on their door one morning or be sent a miniature wooden coffin with the Cross of Lorraine upon it meant to discourage any thoughts of collaboration. After the Allied landings the Resistance attempted to eliminate potential informers to ensure there was a smooth path towards liberation. The proprietor of the *Café du Nord*, known as *Matteo* (the café still stands in the town square next to the abbey), was executed by the Resistance during this period, suspected of having furnished the Germans with the list of people who were rounded up on February 14th and which had caused such terrible heartache. He was not missed in Cluny. Collaborators, *milicians* and captured German soldiers were all executed in Cluny and its environs during this period of 'wild cleansing'.

It is difficult to know how many *femmes tondues* 'shorn women' there were in Cluny and its environs, where women's heads were shaved as punishment for what was known as 'horizontal collaboration'. Martinerie says that it 'is not a subject which brings honour to the Resistance'. That it happened in Cluny is evidenced by a photograph in his book which shows three women with their heads shaved, standing beside smiling soldiers amid the rubble from the bombardment.(8)

Martinerie is also of the opinion that the unofficial tribunals of the Resistance did the work of the (as he sees it) failing Courts of Justice. 300 suspected collaborators from throughout the department were tried by the official courts: of those 150 cases were dismissed, 50 were fined or spent a short time in prison, only 15, however, were executed. This was no doubt in line with de Gaulle's wish to unite the country as soon as possible but it was also difficult for the Resistance to initially accept after witnessing so many atrocities by the Germans and their accomplices. Sometimes it appears there was a duality of roles between the representative of de Gaulle's government, the *commissaires* and *préfets* and the Resistance Liberation Committees. There was, however, no insurrection or threat to order as had been feared by the central authorities. Often documents were co-signed by government representatives and the local Resistance Committees. (9)

Two memories stand out for the men and women of Cluny: one was of the part played by the Resistance in the liberation of France and to which General Eisenhower paid fulsome tribute.(10) The other was of the achievement of a seamless civil takeover after the Liberation. "Within 48 hours of the last German fleeing a town or area, administrators were in place, food and fuel were available, the *Préfecture* ran smoothly. This was the stunning legacy of Jean Moulin. (11)

In March 1944 the united Resistance movements under the National Council of the Resistance drew up a post-war programme of action. The first half concerned the course of immediate action, including how to deal with collaborators; the second concerned measures to be taken to secure 'a more just social order' after the liberation. This second part, known as the Resistance charter, was adopted by all the major political parties before the general election of 1945. (12)

As part of his nation-building project de Gaulle wished to project the image of heroes, not victims. In the face of what they interpreted as official neglect, various associations of *déportés* were set up to keep the memory of their experiences alive. In 1954 the associations succeeded in getting parliament to vote for an annual National Deportation Day every April. "In the hierarchy of virtue in post-war France, the deportees had come to occupy a central place only just below the resisters. They symbolise the sufferings of the French nation during their five years of occupation by an alien force". (13) Many of the children of the deportees of Cluny, now in their 60's and 70's continue to make annual pilgrimages to Mauthausen or Ravensbruck, as they have told us in their testimonies.

In 1952 an association was set up by the deportees and their children: *Les Amicales des Déportés de Cluny* (Friends of the Cluny Deportees). Its purpose was to create a focus for mutual support and also where possible, to ensure financial support for the families of deportees and to support the widows and orphans in families where the wage-earning parent had not returned. They ensure that the important days in their calendar were observed: the National Deportation Day in April and the commemoration of the February 14th round-up, a date engraved forever in the memories of Cluny people. The day takes the form of a church service, followed by a gathering at the deportation monument, which stands opposite the place where those arrested stood throughout that cold February day, hands above their heads, awaiting eventual deportation.

In 2004, sixty years after the round-up, the sons and daughters of the deportees held a commemorative exhibition in a hall near that spot. A commemorative volume was also produced, telling the deportees' story and including testimonies and photographs. The testimonies translated here are from that book. The title they chose came from the comment written by a child of eleven in the exhibition's visitors' book. After seeing the exhibition and learning the story of what happened in her town those sixty years earlier, the child wrote *"Le pire c'est que c'était vrai."* "The worst is that it is all true".

Notes and References

PREFACE

1. Amicale des Déportés de Cluny, *Cluny, Fevrier 1944, 'Le pire c'est que c'était vrai!'* (JPM), 2005

2. Viguié-Moreau, Marie-M, *Les Orphelins de la Saint-Valentin* (Paris : l'Harmattan, 2004)

3. Martinerie, Jean, *Eléments pour une approche historique de La Résistance en Clunysois et Lieux Circonvoisins*, private publication by the Amicale des Déportés de Cluny et du Clunysois, (Beaubery, 2010)

CHAPTER 1: INTRODUCTION: FRANCE AT WAR

1. I am indebted to Roderick Kedward's *La Vie en Bleu: France and the French since 1900* (London: Allen Lane, 2005) for much of this section.

2. It has been said that Gamelin used World War I methods to fight World War II, but with less vigour and slower response. See ***The Collapse of the Third Republic: An Inquiry into the Fall of France in 1940*** by William L. Shirer (New York: Simon and Schuster, 1969) which deals with the collapse of the French Third Republic as a result of Hitler's invasion during World War II.

3. Kedward, pp. 252 – 253.

4. Robert Paxton, *Vichy France: Old Guard and New order, 1940 – 1944* (London: Barrie & Jenkins, 1972), p. 222.

5. Kedward, p. 253.

6. Kedward, p. 249.

7. Text of De Gaulle's speech of 22nd June 1940 from http://lehrmaninstitute.org/history/index.html

8. Matthew Cobb, *The Resistance: The French Fight Against the Nazis* (London: Simon & Schuster, 2010), p. 35).

9. Kedward, p. 288,

10. Paxton, p. 292.

11. Special Operations Executive (S.O.E) was an independent British secret service, set up in July 1940 and disbanded in January 1946. Its task was to co-ordinate subversive and sabotage activity against the enemy and if necessary to initiate it.

12. The principal Resistance movements were: Combat, founded by Henry Frenay in November 1941: Liberation, founded by d'Astier de la Vigerie, Raymond and Lucie Aubrac in July 1941: Franc-Tireur, of communist origin in 1941: l'Organisation de Résistance de l'Armée (Organisation of the Resistance of the Army), 1942. In November 1942 Jean Moulin: ('Rex' or 'Max', who acted as personal envoy to de Gaulle), united these three movements into *Mouvements Unis de la Résistance (MUR*, who recognised de Gaulle as leader. He eventually created (with de Gaulle's blessing) the *Conseil Nationale de la Résistance* (CNR) with oversight of the resistance in both the north and the south. Moulin died after arrest and torture in 1943. (From Kedward p. 292).

13. Kedward, p. 276.

CHAPTER 2: A TOWN AT WAR: CLUNY 1940 - 1945

1. **Gadz'Arts** was the nickname given students from the prestigious Schools of Arts and Engineering (École Nationale Supérieure d'Arts et Métiers). It is a contraction of *Gars des Arts et Métiers*. These schools are the leading engineering schools in the fields of mechanics and industrialization in France. They are now known collectively as the Arts and Métiers Paris Tech (ENSAM) with campuses at Paris, Aix-en-Provence, Angers, Lille, Bordeaux, Châlons-en-Champagne, Cluny and Metz.

2. A few days later, on 22nd June, and as a result of the Armistice and France's capitulation, the German tanks came through the town again – this time in the other direction – back to maintain the occupation of the North leaving the south, the other side of the demarcation line, to the ministrations of the French Vichy Government.

3. The *Mairie* is the equivalent of the Town Hall but which tends to play a far bigger part in the life of village and towns in France than its UK equivalent.

4. *Legion Française des Combattants* **(French Veterans' Legion),** In the inter-war years, many Friends and Veterans Organisations were created. In 1940 Vichy merged all the existing organisation into the *Légion Française des Combattants* (French Veterans' Legion), for propaganda purposes. It was intended to regenerate the nation, by virtue

of the example of the sacrifice of 1914-1918 and to support the Vichy government. In 1943, in response to the growing number of Resistance fighters, it gave rise to the French Militia *(La Milice)*.

5. *La Milice*: The *Milice Française* was a paramilitary force created in January 1943 by the Vichy Regime, with German aid, to help fight the French Resistance. The *milice*'s chief of operations was Joseph Darnand. They participated in summary executions and assassinations, and helped round up the Jews and *résistants* for deportation. They often resorted to torture to extract information or confessions from those they rounded up. They were often considered more dangerous to the French Resistance than the Gestapo and SS since they were Frenchmen who spoke the language, had a full knowledge of the towns and land, and knew people and informers. It appealed to members of the inter-war fascist leagues, to ultra-Catholics and to wealthy young Royalists as well as members of France's pre-war far right-wing parties and also working-class men convinced by Vichy's alliance with Nazi Germany. The organisation "was the mirror of the German Gestapo and which was regarded with repugnance and fear. At its height it counted on some 35,000 volunteers. The Vichy of the *milice* was a veritable police state. It was comparable to any European fascism." (Kedward, p.271). The struggle between the *maquis* and the *milice* in some regards had an appearance of a civil war.

6. **The Prefect** was Monsieur Alfred Golliard who was prefect of the Jura *Département* in Eastern France (which

borders Burgundy). He was stripped of office by the Vichy government for refusing to co-operate with the German occupying forces and retired to Cluny. Here he became a member of the Resistance working with the English S.O.E. team 'Buckmaster'. His convictions were known to the local *milice* and also the Gestapo. He was arrested during the raid of 14th February 1944 and died in the Mauthausen-Gusen Concentration Camp on 16th August 1944. In France, a *préfet* is a high-ranking civil servant who represents the State at the level of the *département* or region. One of the many important administrative roles is to ensure that government decisions are carried out at a local level. This Monsieur Golliard could not bring himself to do after the German invasion.

7. Kedward, p. (274).

8. **Special Operations Executive** : was an independent British secret service, set up in July 1940 and disbanded in January 1946. Its task was to co-ordinate subversive and sabotage activity against the enemy and where necessary initiate it. "In every German-occupied country there were spontaneous outbursts of national fury at Nazi rule. SOE's objects included discovering where these outbursts were, encouraging them when they were feeble, arming their members as they grew, and coaxing them when they were strong into the channels of greatest common advantage to the allies." (Foot, p. xvii). "The Resistance groups that SOE nurtured in France secured over a thousand interruptions of rail traffic in a single June week. By the end of the war about

two hundred agents trained by SOE were incarcerated in the German concentration camps. Of those, fewer than forty returned to recount what they had been through". (Foot, p. xxii).

9. Foot, p. 215. **Commander Joseph Marchand** (pseudonym *Arthur)* arrived September 1942 and was the officer in charge of the network *Buckmaster* for the S.O.E (Services Operations Executive) in the area, working from Lyon.

10. **Major Maurice Buckmaster,** formerly a Ford manager in Paris led 'F' section of the S.O.E which set up over 100 circuits in France in which hand-picked agents, smuggled or dropped into the country, recruited and trained groups of *résistants* for military action. A quarter of the four-hundred agents sent out to France did not return. (Kedward, p. 286: Foot, p. 20). After the war he was awarded the French *Croix de Guerre*, the American Legion of Merit and the British OBE.

11. ...*Une zone, ainsi dire franche, qui devra, en principe et dans la mesure du possible être interdite aux excursions ennemies, au moins au travail de la 5e colonne. La région se prête à ces conditions: une ravitaillement facile, une mentalité depuis longtemps travaillée où tout le monde se connaît, donc d'une épuration facile. Dans cette région, il serait reçu et distribué les armes, formé, équipé et instruit des maquis motorisés... les liaisons devraient y être sûres.* (Patrick Veyret, *La Bataille de Cluny: 11th août 1944*).

12. **Captain Brown-Bartoli:** Germaine Moreau recalls: "One of our team, Jean Renaud, met him at the station and took him

home to stay with them. Needing to find him a pseudonym, Jean's wife, Henriette, looking at the calendar saw it was 14 April, St Tiburce's day, thus he became 'Tiburce' or 'Toto' for short!"

13. **Jean Renaud,** one of the instigators and leaders of the Resistance in the Cluny region was arrested 10 June 1944 and 'disappeared'. It is not known what happened to him but there is a strong possibility that he suffered at the hands of Klaus Barbie. Barbie was at this time head of the Gestapo in Lyon where he earned the name the *Butcher of Lyon.* It is estimated that he was directly responsible for the deaths of up to 14,000 people. The most infamous case is the arrest and torture of Jean Moulin, one of the highest-ranking members of the French Resistance. Barbie was identified in Bolivia in 1971, arrested and extradited to France. In 1984 he was put on trial for crimes committed while in charge of the Gestapo in Lyon between 1942 and 1944. Sentenced to life imprisonment for crimes against humanity he died in prison in Lyon four years later at the age of 77.

14. **Letters of denunciation**: during the Vichy era, French residents sent between three and five million denunciation letters. This figure includes both signed and unsigned letters. See André Halimi, *La Délation sous l'Occupation* (Paris: Editions Alain Moreau, 1983).

15. Kedward, pp. 262, 295.

CHAPTER 3: RESISTANCE BEGINS: THE STORY OF GERMAINE AND ANTOINE MOREAU

1. **Henri Frenay** was born into a military family in 1905. He later studied the Germanic languages at the University of Strasbourg. He followed a military career reaching the rank of captain. At the outbreak of World War II, he was captured by the German forces. He escaped from a POW camp in 1940 and made his way to Marseille. He went on to form the French Resistance group *Mouvement de Liberation Nationale* in 1940 and had a hand in the formation of the *Combat* group in November, 1941. Berty Albrecht, although married, left her husband when she met Henri Frenay. They were together for the rest of their lives and worked tirelessly for the Resistance movement, becoming directors of the *Combat* network. Albrecht was arrested by the Gestapo in 1943 and tortured. She committed suicide by hanging. After the war, her body was buried in the crypt of the French Resistance martyrs in Mount Valerien. Henri Frenay died in 1988.

(http://en.wikipedia.org/wiki/Berty_Albrecht)

(http://en.wikipedia.org/wiki/Henri_Frenay)

2. **The School of Army Health (l'Ecole de Santé Militaire)** now known as the Institute of Pharmaceutical and Biological Sciences, Lyon, is the training institution for pharmacists and doctors for the French armed services. The School became the headquarters for the Gestapo during the war. Under the reign

of Klaus Barbie, the cellars became notorious for a place of execution and torture. Jean Moulin was one of its victims.

3. **Fort Montluc** is a former prison located in the 3rd arrondissement of Lyon. Formerly a military prison, after the invasion of the unoccupied zone of Vichy France in November 1942 the Gestapo used it as an interrogation centre and internment camp for those waiting to be transferrd to concentration camps. It is estimated that over 15,000 people were imprisoned in Montluc, and over 900 of them were executed there. Montluc was liberated on 24 August 1944 by FFI troops, when resistance leader Colonel Koenig, profiting from the chaos reigning in Lyon at the time, entered the Fort in a stolen German Army car disguised as a Gestapo officer and persuaded the Commandant to free the prisoners, saying that the order had come from the Gestapo Commander in Lyon, Klaus Barbie. In 2009, most of the prison, including the walls, the stairs and the courtyard, has been classified *monument historique.*

(http://en.wikipedia.org/wiki/Fort_Montluc).

4. **The camp Royallieu (Frontstalag 122)** at Compiègne (Oise, Picardy) was a Nazi transit and internment camp. Over 54,000 *résistants,* political and civil activists, and Jews were interned there. From June 1941 to August 1944 some 54,000 people were interned there, 50,000 of whom were deported to the concentration and extermination camps at Auschwitz, Ravensbrück, Buchenwald, Dachau, Sachsenhausen and Mauthausen.

5. **Romainville:** Fort de Romainville was a Nazi prison and transit camp, located in the outskirts of Paris. The Fort was taken over in 1940 by the German military and transformed into a prison. From there, *resistants* and hostages were directed to the camps. 3,900 women and 3,100 men were interned before being deported to Auschwitz, Ravensbruck, Buchenwald and Dachau concentration camps.

6. *Nacht und Nebel* (Night and Fog) was a directive of Adolf Hitler in 1941 that was intended to winnow out all political activists and resistance 'helpers', 'anyone endangering German security' throughout Nazi Germany's occupied territories. It was later expanded to include all persons in occupied countries who had been taken into custody and were still alive eight days later. The decree was meant to intimidate local populations into submission by denying friends and families any knowledge of the whereabouts or fate of the deportees. The prisoners were secretly transported to Germany, vanishing without a trace. To this day, it is not known how many thousands of people disappeared as a result of this order. http://en.wikipedia.org/wiki/Nacht_und_Nebel.

7. **Jean de Lattre de Tassigny** (1889 – 1952). He was wounded in WW1 and received 8 citations. In March 1939 he took command of the 14th Division of French Infantry who had fought the Germans in 1940. After the Armistice he commanded the 16th Montpelier Division and refused the order from Vichy not to oppose the invasion of the southern 'free' zone in November 1942. Arrested, he went before a tribunal at Lyon and was interned at Mont Luc prison under

French administration until January 1943. He was condemned to 10 years imprisonment. Transferred to a Riom prison, he escaped in September 1943. He joined de Gaulle in London and then Algiers and was promoted to the rank of general by de Gaulle. At the head of the 1st French army, he disembarked in Provence 15th August 1944 and went on to liberate Lyon. He represented France at Berlin at the German capitulation in May 1945. He was given the title of Marshall of France posthumously.

Centre d'Histoire de la Résistance et de la Déportation: ISBN 978 – 2 – 11 – 099542 – 1.

8. **After the war Germaine was awarded:**

Médaille de la Déportation

Médaille de la France libérée 1959

Croix de Guerre avec Palmes 1967

Chevalier de la Légion d'Honneur 1967

Médaille des Combattants Volontaires de la Résistance 1967

Elevée au grade d'Officier de la Légion d'Honneur 1970

Her husband, Antoine Moreau was awarded:

Croix de Guerre avec citation 1946

Médaille de la Résistance 1947

Chevalier de la Légion d'Honneur 1970

CHAPTER 4: A FIANCEE'S STORY: JEAN AND
HENRIETTE ALIX

1. Chantiers de Jeunesse (Youth Work Camps): Young
men of twenty, called up for military service in June 1940 and
numbering roughly 100,000, were overtaken by the defeat.
Pétain then established these young men's work camps
designed to train the erstwhile conscripts to help with
agricultural and forestry work in place of the many French
prisoners of war currently held in German camps.

2. The Vercors Plateau, south-east of Grenoble was the site
of 400 *maquisards*. High up in impregnable mountains it
aimed to be a retrenchment camp for the local Resistance who
had constructed an air field in order to maintain supplies.
Following the Normandy landings of June 1944, they were
joined by more than 4,000 volunteers, assembled there
awaiting the arrival of the Allies. Instead SS commandos
arrived in gliders on 21st July. After three days of hopeless
fighting, the order to with draw was given by the chief of the
maquis. It is said that 20,000 German soldiers annihilated
4,000 French *maquisards.*

3. Mauthausen - Gusen grew throughout the course of the
Second World War to become a large complex of Nazi
Concentration Camps   built around the villages of
Mauthausen and Gusen in Upper Austria, 20 kilometres east
of Linz. It ran from the time of the *Anschluss* in 1938 until the

end of the War. The Gusen Camp was originally called Mauthausen II.

4. **Hôtel Lutetia:** The **Hôtel Lutetia**, St-Germain-de-Près, Paris was used by the Germans after 1940 as a club for officers. After the Liberation it was taken over by the British and American forces and used as a repatriation centre for prisoners of war and returnees from the German concentration camps.

5. See chapter 13 for full details of this reprisal bombing raid.

6. **Phoscao** was a 'fortifying cocoa drink', thought 'to cure anemia, neuresthalgia and stomach problems'.

(http://www.greatwardifferent.com/Great_War/Advertisements/Advertisem ents_Phoscao_01.htm).

CHAPTER 5: A FATHER DEPORTED: THE LARDY FAMILY

1. A **kapo** or **prisoner functionary** (German: *Funktionshäftling*) was a prisoner in a Nazi concentration camp who was assigned by the SS guards to supervise forced labor or carry out administrative tasks in the camp. It minimized costs by allowing camps to function with fewer SS personnel. The system was also designed to turn victim against victim, as the prisoner functionaries were pitted against their fellow prisoners in order to maintain the favor of their SS guards. Many prisoner functionaries were recruited from the ranks of violent criminal gangs and were known for their brutality toward other prisoners. This brutality was

tolerated by the SS and was an integral part of the camp system. (http://en.wikipedia.org/wiki/Kapo_(concentration_camp).

CHAPTER 6: A SON DEPORTED: RENE PERNOT

1. **Royallieu camp (*Frontstalag* 122)** at Compiègne (southeast of Amiens) was a Nazi transit and internment camp from June 1941 to August 1944. The publication in 2008 of the first historical study of the camp revealed its role in the programme of Nazi genocide. More than 54,000 *résistants,* trade unionists, communists, political prisoners, civilians and Jews were held there before being deported to Germany and the extermination camps.

(http://fr.wikipedia.org/wiki/Camp_de_Royallieu)

2. **During an American bombing** raid on 24th August was directed at a nearby armament factory, several bombs, including incendiaries also fell on the camp resulting in heavy casualties amongst the prisoners. (2,000 prisoners wounded and 388 killed by the raid).

⁽http://en.wikipedia.org/wiki/Buchenwald_concentration_camp.)

CHAPTER7: A BYSTANDER'S STORY: ROBERT CHANUT

1.**Nikolaus 'Klaus' Barbie** (1913 – 1991) was an SS-*Hauptsturmführer* (rank approximately equivalent to army captain), Gestapo member and war criminal. He was known as the Butcher of Lyon. In 1942, he was assigned to Lyon as the head of the local Gestapo at the age of 29. After the war he was recruited by the Western Allies and worked for the

British until 1947 and then the U.S. Army Counter Intelligence Corps. In 1951, he fled to Argentina with the help of the U.S. intelligence services, living under the alias Klaus Altmann. In 1971 Barbie was identified as living in Bolivia in 1971 by the Klarsfelds, (Nazi hunters from France). He was extradited to France in 1983 to stand trial. He was indicted for crimes committed while he directed the Gestapo in Lyon between 1942 and 1944. He was tried on 41 separate counts of crimes against humanity, based on the depositions of 730 Jews and resistance fighters, who cited his torture practices and murders. In 1987 he was convicted and sentenced to life imprisonment. He died in prison in Lyon of leukaemia four years later, at the age of 77.

(http://en.wikipedia.org/wiki/Klaus_Barbie).

2. **The French Aerostatic Corps** or Company of Aeronauts (French: *compagnie d'aérostiers*) was the world's first air force, founded in 1794 to use balloons, primarily for reconnaissance.

3. **These clogs, called *galoches*** by Monsieur Chanut, were a type of shoe commonly worn in rural settings at this time. They had canvas or leather tops and a sole carved of wood. The term may trace back to the Middle Ages, from the Gaulish shoe or *gallicae*. When the Romans conquered Gaul (France), they borrowed the Gaulish boot style. The term originally referred to wooden shoes or patten, or merely a wooden sole fastened to the foot by a strap or cord.

(http://en.wikipedia.org/wiki/Galoshes)

4. **Badges of various colours were** worn by the deportees in German labour camps to denote nationality, status etc. A green triangle with the tip pointing down was worn by criminals who were employed by the SS to control the inmates.

(http://d-d.natanson.pagesperso-orange.fr/triangles.htm).

5. **The red triangle** was worn by French political prisoners, communists, resisters etc.

(http://d-d.natanson.pagesperso-orange.fr/triangles.htm).

6. "**As a resident of many camps,** I can say that Gusen was the worst. This is not to say that the conditions at the other camps were not dreadful. Compared to Gusen, however, one might almost say that those camps were paradises. The proof of this might be that Gusen was one of the least known camps. This was not because it was smaller than the others - it might even have been the largest. It was unknown simply because very few of the tens of thousand of prisoners sent there remained alive to tell the story of its horrors."

(Rabbi Rav Yechezekel Harfenes (when back to Auschwitz) in "BeKaf HaKela" (Slingshot of Hell), Targum Press, Southfield Michigan, 1988 at http://www.gusen.org/.

7. **This account of Monsieur Chanut's** liberation and repatriation is taken from his testimony as recounted to the Museum of Deportation and Resistance, Besancon.

CHAPTER 8: A SECRET AGENT'S ESCAPE: THE STORY OF CAPTAIN CAYOTTE

1. **Seminarian**: Catholic priest-in-training
2. **Hurigny** is a village in the Saone-et-Loire region of Burgundy, near Macon.
3. **The Prado** is a Catholic association started in 1860 by Father Antoine Chevrier in Lyon to offer spiritual and physical help to poor children and young people leaving prison. It continues to work with vulnerable children and adults offering sports and cultural activities as well as a Catholic education. There is a seminary in Lyon which prepared young men for this ministry. This young man was a student at the seminary in Belley in Burgundy.
4. **Thoiry** is a town in the Haut-Jura region near the Swiss frontier and Lake Geneva.
5. *Bureau du Chiffre*: The Code Breaking Section of the French Intelligence Service.

CHAPTER 9: THE ORPHANS OF ST VALENTINE'S DAY: MARIE-M VIGUIE-MOREAU

1. Marie-M. Viguié-Moreau, *Les orphelins de la Saint-Valentin* (Paris : L'Harmattan, 2004).

CHAPTER 10: A FAMILY BETRAYED: THE BELOT FAMILY

1. *Restos du Coeur:* a charity set up to provide food for destitute or homeless people during winter. They still exist in France.

2. **See Chapter 13** for a full account of this German reprisal raid. Their intention was to destroy the Resistance forces in the area.

3. **Spinning Mill** Jeanine says that it was a mill for *la filature de crin* or horse hair, much used in former times for making mattresses.

4. **A reversion pension** was designed to guarantee the surviving member of a couple a decent standard of living by paying the widow a part of a principal pension which the deceased spouse received or should have received.

5. *Les Pupilles de la Nation* (National Pupils) was launched in 1917 for child victims of war. To families left without a breadwinner it offered extra financial support.

CHAPTER 11: A GENDARME'S STORY: THE PAUTET FAMILY

1. **The French police forces** are organised differently in France than in the UK. There are three main divisions. The National Gendarmerie which is a branch of the French Armed Forces, in charge of public safety among the civilian population. It works principally in rural and suburban areas and in some smaller towns. The National Police (*la Police Nationale)* who operate mostly in large cities and towns, conducting security operations (patrols, traffic control, identity checks and also criminal enquiries.The Republican Security Services *(Les CompagniesRépublicaines de Sécurité,* CRS) are the riot control forces. The task for which they are

best known is crowd and riot control and re-establishment of order.

2. **Georges Loustaunau-Lacau** (1894–1955) was a French army officer, anti-communist conspirator, resistant, and politician. An officer of extreme right-wing with anti-communist views, he was one of the founders of a right-wing military organisation, the *Union des Comités d'action défensive*. His complicity with this organisation was discovered and he was dismissed from the army in 1938. He was recalled to active service on the outbreak of the Second World War, but was arrested in 1940 and imprisoned. Later in 1940, under Pétain's new Vichy regime, he was appointed to head the Légion française des combattants, a veteran's organisation created by the regime. He used his new post as a cover to recruit agents for a resistance organisation, known as the Alliance network. He was later arrested and deported to Mauthausen Concentration Camp. He survived his imprisonment and after the war entered conventional politics. He published *Chiens Maudits* (Accursed Dogs), his memoirs of the Nazi Labour Camps (Paris, Editions Network Alliance, 1960, 96 pp).

(http://en.wikipedia.org/wiki/Georges_Loustaunau-Lacau).

3. **Marie-Louis Zimberlin** was a teacher at Cluny Technical College. Arrested on February 14th, she was deported to Ravensbruck. After having been liberated, she died during the return journey near Geneva on 14th May 1945. She was awarded the *Chevalier de la Legion d'honneur* and the *Croix de Guerre* posthumously in June 1947.

224

4. **After his death** his wife found the following awards among his papers:

- Award of the National Order of the *Légion d'Honneur au grade de chevalier* in March 1957
- The Medal of the *Résistance Française*
- Certificate of the *Forces Françaises Combattantes* of the Tiburce- Buckmaster Network from 1st March 1943 to 1 September 1942 as agent P.I.C.M. 3 grade sub-lieutenant
- Certificate for his action as part of the Forces Françaises de l'Intérieur established by Captain Moreau of Cluny against the occupying Germans.

CHAPTER 12: A NURSE'S STORY: MARIE-ANGELY REBILLARD

1.**Monsieur Henri Nigay**, born 30th January 1893, father of five, was arrested in his café-restaurant on 14th February 1944 and died in the concentration camp at Mauthausen 7th November 1944.

2. *Haras National de Cluny:* The Cluny Stud Centre is renowned for its purebred stallions and high-quality racehorses. In 1806 Napoleon 1st ordered the creation of 30 breeding farms across the nation which included the stable at Cluny

3. **Mademoiselle Rebillard** uses the term 'le tambour de ville' (the town drum) and there is a picture of the Cluny towncrier, Monsieur 'Kiki' Bernard with his cart, drums and bells. http://fr.wikipedia.org/wiki/Tambour_de_ville says: 'le

tambour de ville' was a town crier who made announcements: he moved through the town, stopping in certain places, his presence was signalled by a call sound (drum, bugle trumpet). People then gathered to listen.

4. **L'Armée Secrète**, the Secret Army, created in 1943 was an organisation of French Resistance fighters set up by Jean Moulin. It was the result of the amalgamation of three smaller Resistance groups (Combat; Libération-Sud; Franc-Tireur), and also former French military personnel in active resistance against the German occupiers. It operated mainly in the south of France. From 1944 it became known as the French Forces of the Interior as D-Day drew nearer.

5 **Fourteen** *Clunyois* died in the German bombardment of 11th August 1944, including Sister Isabelle.

CHAPTER 13: THE BATTLE FOR CLUNY AUGUST 11TH 1944

1. **I am grateful** to the following for information on the battle for Cluny:

- *Cluny "La Résistante": La bataille du 11 Aout 1944,* unpublished account by General Loizillon
- *La Bataille de Cluny: Les maquis de Saône-et-Loire mettent en échec la Freiwilligen-Stamm-Division,* unnamed magazine article by Patrick Veyret
- *Cluny, Février 1944: Le Pire c'est que c'était vrai* by l'Amicale des Déportés de Cluny
- http://actl.forumgratuit.org/t284-la-bataille-de-cluny:

2. *Sédentaires* was the name given to trained members of the resistance who, unlike the *maquis* (who lived under cover in the woods and hills), carried on their daily lives whilst waiting to be called for active involvement.

3. **After 'D-Day' the Resistance**, together with the *Maquis* changed its name to become the 'French Forces of the Interior' (*Forces Francaise de l'Intérieur).* Charles de Gaulle used it as a formal name for the resistance fighters. The change in designation of these groups to FFI occurred as France's status changed from that of an occupied nation to one of a nation being liberated by the Allied armies. As regions of France were liberated, the FFI were more formally organized into light infantry units and served as a valuable manpower addition to regular French forces. FFI units seized bridges, began the liberation of villages and towns as Allied units neared, and collected intelligence on German units in the areas entered by the Allied forces, easing the Allied advance through France in August 1944. On 20 June 1944, the French high command decreed the mobilization requirements dating from the start of the war were still in effect, that the FFI units were to be made part of the French Army, and that the FFI was subject to French military law.

(http://en.wikipedia.org/wiki/French_Forces_of_the_Interior).

4. **The French Secret Army** (L'armée secréte) was the name given to the amalgamation of three Resistance groups, Combat. Liberation, Franc-Tireur, brought about by Jean Moulin before his death in 1943 and mainly operative in the

south of France. After 1944 it became part of the FFI (see note I above).

(http://en.wikipedia.org/wiki/Arm_secrete).

5. **Freiwilligen-Stamm-Division** was formed in January 1944 in southern France and was used to train units made up of volunteers from the USSR. It saw action against the French resistance. Soldiers from this division were among the 80 German POWs killed by French partisans at Les Rousses 3 September 1944 in reprisal of the killing of French civilians (http://www.axishistory.com/index).

6. **Laurent Bazot**: "Commandant Laurent Bazot, Army of France, was awarded the Distinguished Service Cross for extraordinary heroism in connection with military operations against an armed enemy while serving with the 4th Battalion de Choc, in action against the enemy forces on 31 March 1945. Commandant Bazot's outstanding accomplishments, personal bravery and zealous devotion to duty exemplify the highest traditions of the Armed Forces of the Allied Nations" *militarytimes.com/citations-medals-awards/recipient.*

7. **"On its way north,** the SS *Reich* division carved out for itself a private niche in the book of iniquity. Its mens' tempers had worn exceedingly thin. It had been held up at one point on the Dordogne … and sniped at incessantly when passing through villages and small towns as in open country …holdups of this kind naturally assisted the RAF. A popular company commander was killed in a village called Oradour-sur Vayres, 25 miles west of Limoges. For his death the Germans extracted a price all the more extraordinary for being

levied on the wrong villages – Oradour-sur-Glane, fifteen miles away. ...and so the name of Oradour has joined the names in the blackest catalogue of men's treatment of man. The massacre illustrates the same lesson as at Vercors: how German troops much subjected to guerrilla treatment ceased to behave in accordance with what are curiously known as 'the laws' of war'." Foote p. 399.

CHAPTER 14: LIBERATION

1. **Jackson,** p.529

2. **Joseph Darnand,** 1897-1945. After service in the First World War, he joined a number of right-wing political, paramilitary and terrorist organizations: l'Action Francaise in 1925; les Croix-de-Feu in 1928; la Cagoule and Jacques Doriot's Parti Populaire Francaise in 1936. After the armistice he took a leading position in the Vichy sanctioned Légion Française des combattants (French Legion of Veterans). Unhappy with the LFC's moderation, he formed the Service d'Ordre Légionnaire (SOL) to take direct and violent action against the enemies of Marshal Petain's National Revolution. The SOL gained official recognition as *la Milice Francaise* on 1st January , 1943 which Darnard led. He took the SS oath of allegiance to Hitler in October 1943. He fled into Germany one step ahead of the Allied advance. The remnants of the *Milice* were integrated with the SS Charlemagne Division that guarded Hitler's bunker during the final days of the Third Reich. Darnand was arrested shortly after the war, tried by the

High Court, sentenced to death and executed on 10th October , 1945. http://worldatwar.net/biography/d/darnand/.

3. **Jackson,** p. 530.

4. **Jackson,** p. 531.

5. **On the 8th May this division,** on their way north, reached Tulle in the Correze. It has recently been declared liberated by a group of *maquisards* . They hanged ninety-nine men of the town from the balconies in the main street on 9th June. On 10 June a battalion of the division arrived at the village of Oradour-sur-Glane, a small market town. Mistaking this Oradour for another a short distance away the women and children were rounded into the church which they then burned. The men were rounded up and machine gunned. 642 people died that day.

6. **Richard Vinen,** *The Unfree French: Life under the Occupation* (Penguin, London: 2006), pp.328–9.

7. **Jackson,** p.541.

8. **14th July** or *Le quatorze juillet* is a day of national celebration in France, commemorating as it does the storming of the Bastille prison, in Paris on 14th July 1789, seen as a symbol of the uprising or liberation of the people from oppression. Celebratory festivities and official ceremonies are held all over France.

9. **Jean de Lattre de Tassigny** (1889–1952) commanded the 14th French Infantry Regiment prior to the armistice. He accepted the armistice and remained on active duty in Tunisia and Algeria. He landed in Provence on16th August 1944, liberated Toulon and Marseilles with the First French Army

where he joined General Patch's American troops in the march up the Rhone Valley and met Leclerc's 2nd Armoured Division on 13th September. He paused to direct the incorporation of resistance fighters into his army before it engaged the Germans in the Battle of Alsace in January 1945. His army crossed the Rhine and Danube reaching the Arlberg Pass in the Tyrolean Alps by war's end. He represented France at the formal German surrender in Berlin on May 9, 1945. He commanded French troops in Vietnam until 1951 when illness forced his return to France. He died in January 1952 and was made Marshal of France posthumously.

(http://worldatwar.net/biography/l/lattre/index.html).

CHAPTER 15: RETURN AND AFTERMATH

1. *Cluny, February 1944,* p.288.

2. Jackson, p.2.

3. The film showed a series of interviews with Resistance fighters, Germans and collaborators. Commenting on the nature and reasons for collaboration they included anti-Semitism; Anglophobia; fear of the Bolsheviks or a Soviet invasion; the desire for power; simple caution.

4. Jenkins, p.201.

5. Four different kinds of courts were set up to judge alleged collaborators. The High Court to judge the cases of Vichy ministers and secretary-generals: the Courts of Justice to deal with other cases of collaboration: the Civic Courts for less serious cases of unpatriotic behaviour which were not technically crimes: there were also military

tribunals which dealt with collaborators before the other courts started to operate. Jackson, p. 577.

6. Ibid. p.577

7. Jenkins, p 215.

8.Jean Martinerie, *Eléments pour une approche historique de La Résistance en Clunysois et Lieux Circonvoisins*, private publication by the Amicale des Déportés de Cluny et du Clunysois, (Beaubery, 2010), p.284.

9. Jackson, p 573-4.

10. General Eisenhower 31st May 1945: ".in no previous war, and in no other theatre during this war, have resistance forces been so closely harnessed to the main military effort. (...) I consider that the disruption of enemy rail communications, the harassing of German road moves and the continual strain placed on the German war economy and internal security service throughout occupied Europe by the organised forces of resistance, played a very considerable part in our complete and final victory". Quoted in Jenkins p. 217.

11. Jenkins, p.212.

12.These measures included more nationalisation and state control of sources of energy, mineral wealth, insurance companies and large banks, readjustment of wages upwards, a plan of social security and restoration of universal suffrage. From Thomson, David, *Democracy in France since 1870* ((London: Oxford University Press, 1964), p 322.

13. Jackson, p 611.

BIBLIOGRAPHY

PRIMARY TEXTS

Amicale des Déportés de Cluny, *Cluny, Fevrier 1944* (JPM), 2005

Viguié-Moreau, Marie-M, *Les Orphelins de la Saint-Valentin* (Paris: l'Harmattan, 2004)

Martinerie, Jean, *Eléments pour une approche historique de La Résistance en Clunysois et Lieux Circonvoisins*, private publication by the Amicale des Déportés de Cluny et du Clunysois, (Beaubery, 2010)

SECONDARY TEXTS

Jenkins, Ray, *A Pacifist at War* (London: Arrow Books, 2010)

Cobb, Matthew, *The Resistance: The French Fight Against the Nazis* (London: Simon & Schuster, 2010)

Foot, M.R.D, *The History of the Second World War: the S.O.E in France* (London: HMSO, 1966)

Gough, Hugh and John Horne, (eds.), *De Gaulle and Twentieth Century France* (London: Edward Arnold, 1994)

Grimbert, Philippe, *Un Secret* (Paris: Grasset & Fasquelle, 2004)

Hoover Institute on War, Revolution and Peace (corporate author), *La Vie de la France sous L'Occupation, (1940 – 1944),* 3 vols, (Paris: Plon, 1957 : New York: Stanford University Press, 1957)

Humbert, Agnes, *Resistance: Memoirs of Occupied France* (London: Bloomsbury, 2008)

Jackson, Julian, *France, The Dark Years, 1940 – 1944* (Oxford: Oxford University Press, 2001)

Jackson, Julian, *The Fall of France: The Nazi Invasion of 1940* (Oxford: Oxford University Press, 2003)

Joffo, Joseph, *Un Sac de Billes* (Paris: Librairie Générale Français, 2005)

Kedward, H.R, *Occupied France: Collaboration and Resistance, 1940 – 1944* (Oxford: Blackwell, 1985)

Kedward, Roderick & Roger Austin, eds., *Vichy France and the Resistance* (London: Croom Helm, 1985)

Kedward, Roderick, *La Vie en Bleu: France and the French since 1900* (London: Allen Lane, 2005)

Kedward, Roderick, *In Search of the Maquis: Rural Resistance in Southern France, 1942 – 1944* (Oxford: The Clarendon Press, 1993)

Jenkins, Cecil: *France: People. History and Culture* (Philadelphia: Running Press Book Publishers, 2011)

McMillan, James F., *Twentieth Century France: Politics and Society 1898 – 1991* (London: Arnold, 1992)

Musée des Beaux-Arts de Chartres (eds), *Jean Moulin, Premier Combat à Chartres* (Chartres: Musée des Beaux-Arts de Chartres,1990)

Némirovsky, Irène, *Suite Française* (Paris: Editions Denoël, 2004)

Ousby, Ian, *Occupation: The Ordeal of France 1940 – 1944* (London: John Murray, 1997)

234

Price, Roger, *A Concise History of France* (Cambridge: Cambridge University Press, 2005)

Paxton, Robert, *Vichy France: Old Guard and New order, 1940 – 1944* (London: Barrie & Jenkins, 1972)

Riding, Alan, *And the Show Went On: Cultural Life in Nazi-Occupied Paris* (London: Duckworth Overlook, 2012)

Sabatier, Robert, *Olivier, 1940* (Paris: Michel Albin, 2003)

Sartre, Jean-Paul, 'La République du silence' in *Situations III* (Paris: Gallimard, 1949)

Shirer,William L., *The Collapse of the Third Republic: An Inquiry into the Fall of France in 1940* (New York: Simon and Schuster, 1969)

Thomson, David, *Democracy in France since 1870* (London, Oxford University Press, 1964)

Tournoux, J-R, *Pétain and De Gaulle,* trans. by Oliver Coburn (London: Heinemann, 1966)

Vercors, *Le Silence de la Mer* (Paris, Michel Albin, 1951: first published Paris: Librairie Génerale Français, 1944)

Vercors, trans. Rita Barisse, *The Battle for Silence* (London: Collins, 1968)

Vinen, Richard, *The Unfree French: Life under the Occupation* (London: Penguin, 2007)

Williams, Charles, *Pétain* (London: Little, Brown, 2005)

APPENDIX

Biographical Details of the Deportees with details of all arrests

Arrests between 13th September 1943 and 22nd February 1944

	Arrested	Returned	Deceased
Women of Cluny	19	18	1
Women non-domiciled	2	1	1
Men of Cluny	45	15	30
Men non-domiciled	10	1	9

Communes	Arrests	Commentary
CLUNY	76	
BERZE LA VILLE	3	*74 died during deportation*
BLANOT	5	*All died during deportation*
BUSSIERES	2	*Returned*
CORMATIN	5	*Returned except for J. Mercier*
LOURNAND	1	*Died during deportation*
PIERRECLOS	1	*Returned*
SAINT GENGOUX le NLE	3	*Returned*
SALORNAY sur GUYE	1	*Died during deportation*
total	97	

BIOGRAPHIES

Deportees still living in 2004

 **Suzanne BURDIN**	Née Perrin le 11/01/1907 A Mancey S&L Commerçante Arrêtée le 14/02/1944 Déportée « NN » à Ravensbrück/Mauthausen Libérée le 22/04/1945
 **Antoine GUILLOTIN**	Né le 19/11/1915 A Lournand (S&L) Employé Ecole Arts et Métiers Arrêté le 15/02/1944 Déporté à Auchwitz et Büchenwald Libéré le 11/04/1945
 **Robert CHANUT**	Né le 11/07/1924 A Sainte Cécile (S&L) Ajusteur Arrêté le 14/02/1944 Déporté Mauthausen / Gusen Libéré le 05/05/1945

237

 **Raymond JUILLARD**	Né le 19/03/1926 A Bussières (S&L) Arrêté le 27/08/1943 Déporté à Buchenwald, Ohrdruf, Sachenhausen, Bergen Belsen, Hambourg, Neuengamme, Spalding- Strass, Sand-Bostel Libéré le 07/05/1945
 **Georgette COLIN**	Née le15/04/1913 A Vescours (Ain) Commerçante Arrêté le 14/02/1944 Déportée à Ravensbrück- Holleischen Libérée le 05/05/1945
 **Abbé Jean MERCIER**	Né le 09/07/1921 A Mesvres (S&L) Prêtre Arrêté le 05/01/1944 Déporté à Neuen Bremm Prison Frankenthal Libéré le 01/04/1945
Roger DUPLESSIS	Né le 03/04/1924 A Pressy sous Dondin (S&L) Mécanicien Arrêté le 22/04/1944 Déporté à Dachau Libéré le 27/04/1945

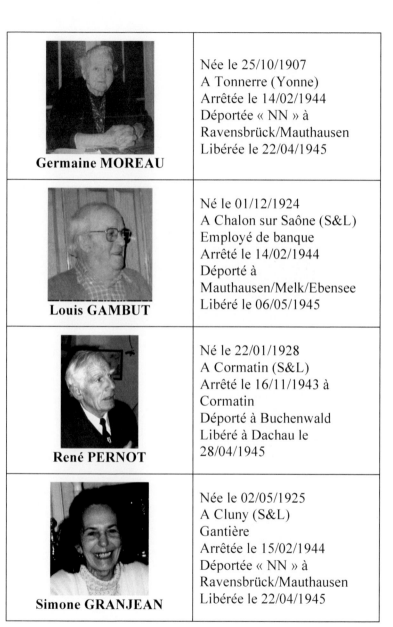

Germaine MOREAU	Née le 25/10/1907 A Tonnerre (Yonne) Arrêtée le 14/02/1944 Déportée « NN » à Ravensbrück/Mauthausen Libérée le 22/04/1945
Louis GAMBUT	Né le 01/12/1924 A Chalon sur Saône (S&L) Employé de banque Arrêté le 14/02/1944 Déporté à Mauthausen/Melk/Ebensee Libéré le 06/05/1945
René PERNOT	Né le 22/01/1928 A Cormatin (S&L) Arrêté le 16/11/1943 à Cormatin Déporté à Buchenwald Libéré à Dachau le 28/04/1945
Simone GRANJEAN	Née le 02/05/1925 A Cluny (S&L) Gantière Arrêtée le 15/02/1944 Déportée « NN » à Ravensbrück/Mauthausen Libérée le 22/04/1945

 **Marius THERVILLE**	Né le 30/11/1908 A Saint Micaud (S&L) Bourrelier Arrêté le 16/11/1943 Déporté à Buchenwald-Weimar Libéré le 23/04/1945
 **Jeannette DILLENSINGER**	Née le 28/05/1921 A Breitenbach (Bas Rhin) Employée d'hôtel Arrêtée le 14/02/1944 Déportée à Ravensbruck / Holleichen Libérée le 05/05/1945
 **Raymond THEVENET**	Né le 01/08/1919 A Pierreclos (S&L) Viticulteur Arrêté à Prissé le 27/08/1943 Déporté à Buchenwald, Dora ,Ellrich, Bergen Belsen Libéré le 15/05/1945
 **Simone TAILLANDIER**	Née le 22/09/1919 A Saint Germain en Laye (Yvelines) Sans profession Arrêtée le 14/02/1944 Déportée à Ravensbrück / Mauthausen Libérée le /04/1945

Marcel LATHELIER

Né le 01/02/1912
A Commenailles (Jura)
Primeur
Arrêté le 14/02/1944
Déporté à Mauthausen / Linz

Deportees deceased since their return

Lucien ANCIAN	Né le 09/07/1921 A Thezillieu (Ain) Opticien Arrêté le 01/03/1944 Déporté à Görlitz Libéré le 23/04/1945 Décédé en 2001
René DUBOST	Né le 19/07/1923 A Bussières de Ste Thérence (Allier) Etudiant en pharmacie Célibataire Arrêté au domicile en avril 1944 déporté à Dachau libéré en avril 1945 décédé en 1957

Clunisois who died during deportation

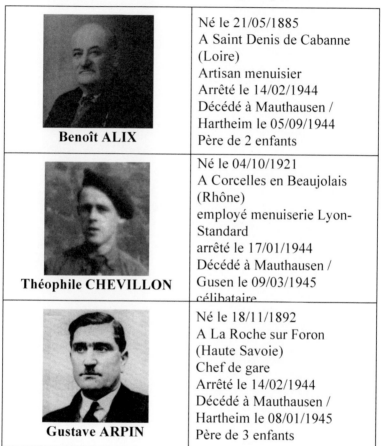

Benoît ALIX	Né le 21/05/1885 A Saint Denis de Cabanne (Loire) Artisan menuisier Arrêté le 14/02/1944 Décédé à Mauthausen / Hartheim le 05/09/1944 Père de 2 enfants
Théophile CHEVILLON	Né le 04/10/1921 A Corcelles en Beaujolais (Rhône) employé menuiserie Lyon-Standard arrêté le 17/01/1944 Décédé à Mauthausen / Gusen le 09/03/1945 célibataire
Gustave ARPIN	Né le 18/11/1892 A La Roche sur Foron (Haute Savoie) Chef de gare Arrêté le 14/02/1944 Décédé à Mauthausen / Hartheim le 08/01/1945 Père de 3 enfants

 **François DARGAUD**	Né le 18/12/1921 A Cluny (S&L) Typographe Arrêté le 17/01/1944 Décédé à Mauthausen / Gusen le 18/12/1944 Célibataire
 **François BAURY**	Né le 06/07/1901 A Cluny (S&L) Facteur Arrêté le 14/02/1944 Décédé à Mauthausen / Gusen le 02/02/1945 Père de 2 enfants
 **Marcel DELCAIRE**	Né le 11/02/1908 A Saint Victour (Corrèze) garagiste Arrêté le 14/02/1944 Décédé à Buchenwald/ Flossenburg le 30/04/1944 Père de 2 enfants
 **Jean-Baptiste BEAUFORT**	Né le 13/03/1878 A Cluny (S&L) Restaurateur hôtelier Arrêté le 14/02/1944 Décédé à Mauthausen/ Hartheim le 22/08/1944 Père de 4 enfants

 **Joseph DEMONFAUCON**	Né le 27/12/1872 A Chatel-Moron (S&L) Pharmacien Arrêté le 14/02/1944 Décédé à Neuengamme le 08/12/1944 Père de 3 enfants
 **André BELOT**	Né le 04/12/1904 à Saint André le Désert (S&L) Chauffeur usine à gaz Arrêté le 14/02/1944 Décédé à Mauthausen / Gusen le 25/08/1944 Père de 5 enfants
 **Pierre FOUILLIT**	Né le 03/05/1887 A Chassagne (Haute Loire) Employé S.N.C.F. Arrêté le 14/02/1944 Décédé à Mauthausen / Hartheim le 16/08/1944 Père de 1 enfant
 **Jean BONAT**	Né le 24/06/1901 A La Folatière (Isère) Garde-champêtre Arrêté le 14/02/1944 Décédé à Mauthausen / Gusen le 03/12/1944 Père de 2 enfants

**Alfred GOLLIARD**	Né le 07/11/1881 A Bourg en Bresse (Ain) *Préfet* (révoqué par Vichy) Arrêté le 14/02/1944 Décédé à Mauthausen / Hartheim le 16/08/1944 Père de 3 enfants
**Jean-Louis GRANDJEAN**	Né le 22/05/1890 A Gibles (S&L) Employé usine à gaz Arrêté le 14/02/1944 Décédé à Mauthausen/ Hartheim le 17/08/1944 Père de 2 enfants
**Claudius MANGEARD**	Né le 08/11/1885 A Chalon sur Saône (S&L) Représentant en lingerie Arrêté le 13/09/1943 Décédé à Buchenwald/ Dora le 30/08/1944 Père de 2 enfants
**Jacques GUERITAINE**	Né le 15/07/1874 A Prissé (S&L) Retraité S.N.C.F. Maire de Cluny Arrêté le 14/02/1944 Décédé à Neuengamme/ Bergen Belsen le 06/11/1944 père de 2 enfants

André MARTIN	Né le 27/05/1906 A Dreux (Eure et Loire) Cafetier restaurateur Arrêté le 14/02/1944 Décédé à Mauthausen / Gusen Le 09/06/1945
 Joseph LAPLACE	Né le 28/03/1898 A Saint Uruges (S&L) Facteur Arrêté le 14/02/1944 Décédé à Mauthausen / Hartheim le 14/12/1944 Père de 1 enfant
 Antoine MARTIN	Né le 02/11/1896 A Cluny (S&L) Artisan menuisier Arrêté le 14/02/1944 Décédé à Mauthausen Le 13/05/1944 Père de 4 enfants
 Jean LARDY	Né le 19/04/1898 A Saint Pierre Le Vieux (S&L) Employé usine à gaz Arrêté le 14/02/1944 Décédé à Mauthausen / Hartheim le 07/09/1944 Père de 2 enfants

 **Charles MICHEL**	Né le 15/10/1909 A Donzy le National (S&L) charcutier Arrêté le 14/02/1944 Décédé à Mauthausen / Gusen le 22/04/1945 Père de 1 enfant
 **René LAROCHE**	Né le 03/05/1895 à Versailles (Yvelines) Cafetier Arrêté le 14/02/1944 Décédé à Mauthausen Le 20/04/1944
 **Claude MOREAU**	Né le 28/02/1901 A Cluny (S&L) Marchand de vins Arrêté le 14/02/1944 Décédé à Mauthausen / Gusen le 12/04/1945 Père de 6 enfants
 **Georges MALERE**	Né le 13/11/1904 A Cluny (S&L) Chef usine à gaz Arrêté le 14/02/1944 Décédé à Mauthausen / Gusen le 21/03/1945 Père de 2 enfants

Jean-Pierre MUSSETTA	Né le 26/01/1914 A Villeurbanne (Rhône) Professeur ENAM Arrêté le 15/02/1944 Décédé à Mauthausen / Hartheim le 07/08/1944 Père de 1 enfant
 Henri NIGAY	Né le 30/01/1893 A Chiddes (S&L) Cafetier restaurateur Arrêté le 14/02/1944 Décédé à Mauthausen / Hartheim le 07/11/1944 Père de 5 enfants
 Marie-Louise ZIMBERLIN	Née le 01/07/1889 A Saint Just en Chevalet (Loire) Professeur la Prat's et ENAM, célibataire Arrêté le 15/02/1944 Déportée à Ravensbrück Décédée au retour à Annemasse le 14/05/1945
Joanny NOLY	Né le 18/07/1896 A Suin (S&L) Ouvrier agricole Arrêté le 14/02/1944 Décédé à Mauthausen / Hartheim le 07/12/1944 célibataire

 Odette DAUXOIS	Née le 15 février 1925 A Salornay /Guye(S&L) Sténo dactylo,Célibataire Arrêtée le10 mai 1944 Déportée à Ravensbrück / Beendorf Décédée au retour à Kassel Le 26 avril 1945
Emile RIGAUD	Né le 28/12/1890 A Lagarde-Parcol (Vaucluse) Receveur PTT Arrêté le 14/02/1944 Décédé à Mauthausen le 03/06/1944 père de 1 enfant
 Marc PASSOT	Né le 21/05/1905 A Lournand (S&L) Cultivateur Arrêté le 15/02/1944 Décédé à Buchenwald / Flossenburg le 02/11/1944
Georges TERRIER	Né le 02/07/1895 A Béni-Mered (Algérie) Cafetier Arrêté le 14/02/1944 Décédé à Mauthausen Le 05/05/1945 Père de 2 enfants

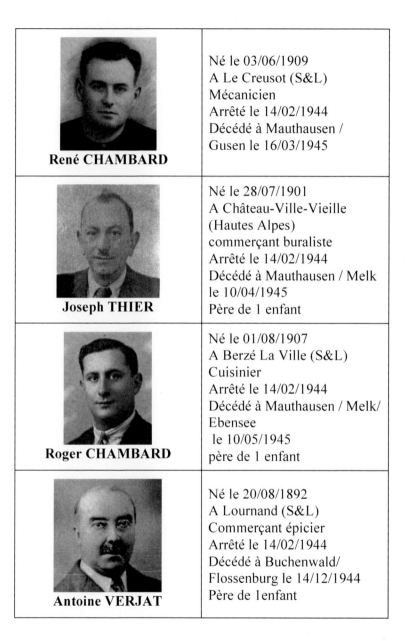

René CHAMBARD	Né le 03/06/1909 A Le Creusot (S&L) Mécanicien Arrêté le 14/02/1944 Décédé à Mauthausen / Gusen le 16/03/1945
Joseph THIER	Né le 28/07/1901 A Château-Ville-Vieille (Hautes Alpes) commerçant buraliste Arrêté le 14/02/1944 Décédé à Mauthausen / Melk le 10/04/1945 Père de 1 enfant
Roger CHAMBARD	Né le 01/08/1907 A Berzé La Ville (S&L) Cuisinier Arrêté le 14/02/1944 Décédé à Mauthausen / Melk/ Ebensee le 10/05/1945 père de 1 enfant
Antoine VERJAT	Né le 20/08/1892 A Lournand (S&L) Commerçant épicier Arrêté le 14/02/1944 Décédé à Buchenwald/ Flossenburg le 14/12/1944 Père de 1enfant

Benoît LITAUDON	Né le 11/07/1888 A Berzé La Ville (S&L) Cultivateur Arrêté le 14/02/1944 Décédé à Mauthausen Le 30/04/1944

Deportees who have died since their return

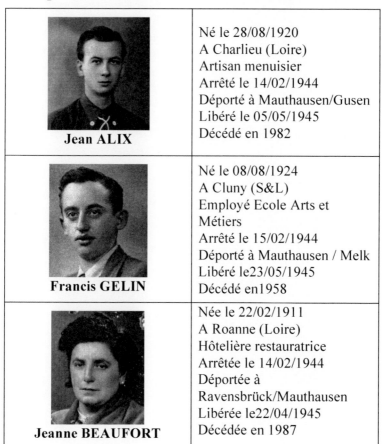

Jean ALIX	Né le 28/08/1920 A Charlieu (Loire) Artisan menuisier Arrêté le 14/02/1944 Déporté à Mauthausen/Gusen Libéré le 05/05/1945 Décédé en 1982
Francis GELIN	Né le 08/08/1924 A Cluny (S&L) Employé Ecole Arts et Métiers Arrêté le 15/02/1944 Déporté à Mauthausen / Melk Libéré le23/05/1945 Décédé en1958
Jeanne BEAUFORT	Née le 22/02/1911 A Roanne (Loire) Hôtelière restauratrice Arrêtée le 14/02/1944 Déportée à Ravensbrück/Mauthausen Libérée le22/04/1945 Décédée en 1987

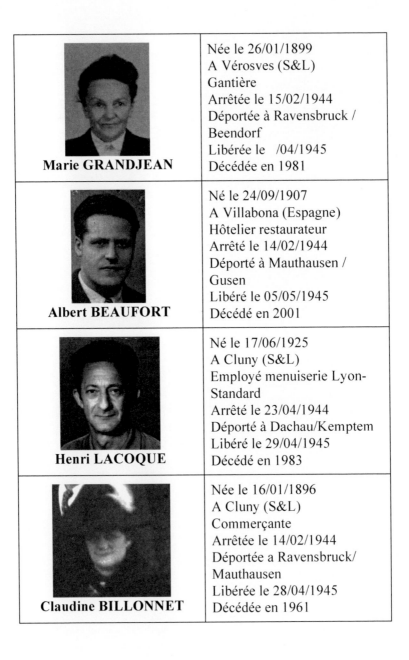

Marie GRANDJEAN	Née le 26/01/1899 A Vérosves (S&L) Gantière Arrêtée le 15/02/1944 Déportée à Ravensbruck / Beendorf Libérée le /04/1945 Décédée en 1981
Albert BEAUFORT	Né le 24/09/1907 A Villabona (Espagne) Hôtelier restaurateur Arrêté le 14/02/1944 Déporté à Mauthausen / Gusen Libéré le 05/05/1945 Décédé en 2001
Henri LACOQUE	Né le 17/06/1925 A Cluny (S&L) Employé menuiserie Lyon- Standard Arrêté le 23/04/1944 Déporté à Dachau/Kemptem Libéré le 29/04/1945 Décédé en 1983
Claudine BILLONNET	Née le 16/01/1896 A Cluny (S&L) Commerçante Arrêtée le 14/02/1944 Déportée a Ravensbruck/ Mauthausen Libérée le 28/04/1945 Décédée en 1961

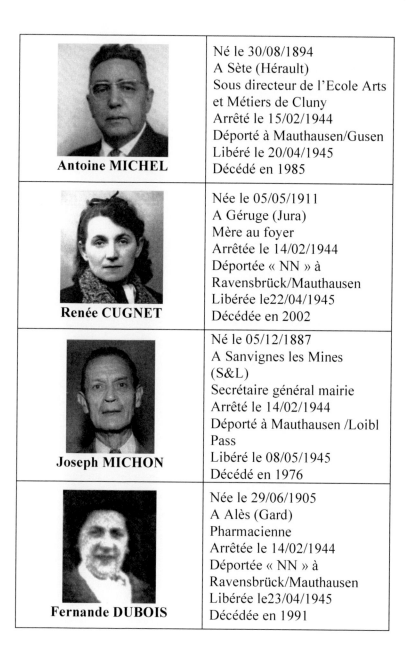

	Né le 30/08/1894 A Sète (Hérault) Sous directeur de l'Ecole Arts et Métiers de Cluny Arrêté le 15/02/1944 Déporté à Mauthausen/Gusen Libéré le 20/04/1945 Décédé en 1985
Antoine MICHEL	
	Née le 05/05/1911 A Géruge (Jura) Mère au foyer Arrêtée le 14/02/1944 Déportée « NN » à Ravensbrück/Mauthausen Libérée le22/04/1945 Décédée en 2002
Renée CUGNET	
	Né le 05/12/1887 A Sanvignes les Mines (S&L) Secrétaire général mairie Arrêté le 14/02/1944 Déporté à Mauthausen /Loibl Pass Libéré le 08/05/1945 Décédé en 1976
Joseph MICHON	
	Née le 29/06/1905 A Alès (Gard) Pharmacienne Arrêtée le 14/02/1944 Déportée « NN » à Ravensbrück/Mauthausen Libérée le23/04/1945 Décédée en 1991
Fernande DUBOIS	

 **Marie PARIZOT**	Née le 19/06/1892 A Jambles (S&L) Commerçante Arrêtée le 14/02/1944 Déportée « NN » à Ravensbrück /Mauthausen Libérée le 22/04/1945 Décédée en 1964
 **Marguerite BARTHELEMY- STRACK**	Née le 08/03/1918 A Cluny (S&L) Sans profession Arrêtée le 13/04/1944 dans le train Déportée à Ravensbrück / Bendorf Décédée en 1979
 **Henriette RENAUD**	Née le 07/02/1905 A Lournand (S&L) Mère au foyer Arrêtée le 14/02/1944 Déportée « NN » à Ravensbrück/Mauthausen Libérée le 22/04/1945 Décédée en 1960
 **Alfred CHARLES**	Né le 22/04/1903 A Cluny (S&L) Couvreur Arrêté le 14/02/1944 Déporté à Mauthausen / Melk Libéré le 05/05/1945 Décédé en 1951

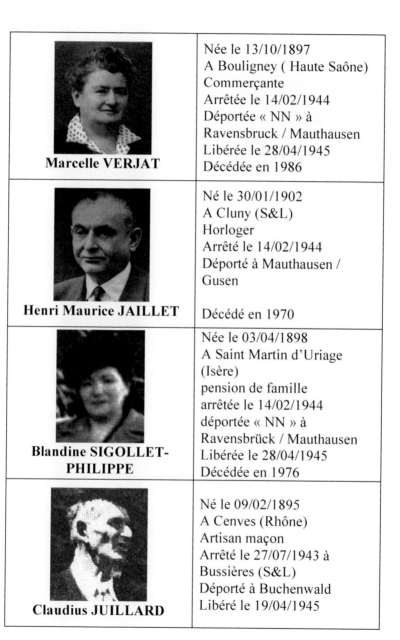

Marcelle VERJAT	Née le 13/10/1897 A Bouligney (Haute Saône) Commerçante Arrêtée le 14/02/1944 Déportée « NN » à Ravensbruck / Mauthausen Libérée le 28/04/1945 Décédée en 1986
Henri Maurice JAILLET	Né le 30/01/1902 A Cluny (S&L) Horloger Arrêté le 14/02/1944 Déporté à Mauthausen / Gusen Décédé en 1970
Blandine SIGOLLET-PHILIPPE	Née le 03/04/1898 A Saint Martin d'Uriage (Isère) pension de famille arrêtée le 14/02/1944 déportée « NN » à Ravensbrück / Mauthausen Libérée le 28/04/1945 Décédée en 1976
Claudius JUILLARD	Né le 09/02/1895 A Cenves (Rhône) Artisan maçon Arrêté le 27/07/1943 à Bussières (S&L) Déporté à Buchenwald Libéré le 19/04/1945

Hélène SAUZET	Née le 08/10/1897 A Cluny (S&L) Agricultrice Arrêtée le 14/02/1944 Déportée « NN » à Ravensbrück / Mauthausen Libérée le 22/04/1945 Décédée en 1974
Claudius PAUTET	Né le 18/02/1900 A Ciry le Noble (S&L) Adjudant de Gendarmerie Arrêté le 30/09/1943 Déporté à Mauthausen / Wiener Neudorf Décédé en 1963
Germaine TERRIER	Née le 25/10/1900 A Montceau-les-Mines (S&L) Commerçante Arrêtée le 14/02/1944 Déportée « NN » à Ravensbrück / Mauthausen Libérée le 28/04/1945 Décédée en 1978
Louis SANSON	Né le 16/11/1895 Arrêté le 14/02/1944 Déporté à Mauthausen Décédé en 1974

Jean-Louis FARGIER

Né le 15/01/1911
A Cormatin (S&L)
Préposé aux PTT
Arrêté le 15/11/1943
Déporté à Buchenwald
Libéré le 24/04/1945
Décédé en1961

Deportees arrested in Cluny but non domiciled

Fernand BACCHARA	
Georges FAVRE	Né le 30/03/1920 A Châtillon de Michaille (Ain) Assurances Arrêté le 14/02/1944 Déporté à Mauthausen /Melk Décédé le 15/02/1945 Célibataire
 Georges COL	Né le 07/10/1917 A Lyon (Rhône) Cuisinier Arrêté le 14/02/1944 Déporté à Mauthausen Décédé le 09/04/1945

Jean Rublio LEPRI	Né le 27/12/1889 A Gubis (Italie) Maçon Arrêté le 14/02/1944 Déporté à Mauthausen Décédé le 29/05/1944 Célibataire
 Georgette COL	Née le 10/06/1919 A Marseille (Bouches du Rhône) Arrêtée le 14/02/1944 Déportée « NN » Ravensbrück / Mauthausen Libérée le /04/1945
 Georges MORLEVAT	Né le 17/02/1909 A Broyes (S&L) Professeur Arrêté le 14/02/1944 Décédé en déportation à Mauthausen /Gusen le 10/03/1945 Père d'un enfant
Daniel COTTE	Né le 22/11/1919 A Lyon (Rhône) Arrêté le 14/02/1944 Déporté à Mauthausen / Melk

Clarisse MORLEVAT	Née le 04/05/1911 A Broyes (S&L) Mère au foyer Arrêtée le 14/02/1944 Décédée en déportation à Ravensbruck le 15/10/1944 Mère d'un enfant
Abbé Pierre DESWARTES	Né le A Prêtre Arrêté le 14/02/1944 en gare de Cluny Déporté à Mauthausen /Melk Décédé le 09/07/1944
Antoine POIVEY	Né le 25/01/1903 A Montceau les Mines (S&L) Manœuvre Arrêté le 14/02/1944 Déporté à Buchenwald / Flossenburg /Hersbruch Décédé le 23/11/1944 Célibataire

POSTSCRIPT
Cluny, September 2013

Mady-M Viguié- Moreau writes:

Tant d'années n'ont pas effacé les souvenirs douloureux des témoins rencontrés par l'auteure. Les liens d'amitié qui se sont tissés lors de ces témoignages prouvent l'écoute exceptionnelle de June Harwood, qui a su comprendre avec émotion et tendresse les histoires d'une époque déjà lointaine mais que nous ne devons pas oublier.

The passage of so many years has not erased the painful memories of those who met the author and told her of their experiences. The ties of friendship which were forged when these testimonies were given are evidence of June Harwood's exceptional gift for listening to others and her ability to understand, with tenderness and emotion, the stories from a time now distant, but which must never be forgotten.

The Bélot Family and Mme Marie Claude Chanraud-Burdin write:

Un groupe d'enfants de Cluny remercie et félicite Madame June Harwood pour le devoir de mémoire que constitue cet ouvrage, hommage aux Clunisois résistants, déportées dans les campes et à toutes les victimes de la barbarie nazie. Quel que soit leur nationalité, June délivre un message aux plus jeunes qui défendent la Liberté: faire en sorte que les horreurs vécues par les familles ne se reproduisent pas. Que le sacrifice des parents ne soit pas vain afin qu'ils connaissent « plus jamais ça ».

A group of 'Children of Cluny' thanks June Harwood and congratulates her for the necessary task of remembrance represented by her work, and for the homage paid, not only to the people of Cluny who resisted and were deported to Nazi camps, but to all victims of Nazi barbarism. This is the message that June sends to all young people who defend freedom, whatever their nationality: act in such a way that the horrors experienced by these families should never occur again and that the sacrifice of their parents should not have been in vain. Never again!